FAITH, LOVE AND FAMILY

Indomitable Spirit of a Mother and her Extraordinary Tale

W0006196

By Rebecca Sandalo Lopez-Golden

PAPERBACK ISBN: 978-1-962905-62-6
HARDCOVER ISBN: 978-1-962905-63-3

ACKNOWLEDGMENT

I am deeply grateful for the invaluable assistance I've received throughout the journey of creating this memoir. I would like to extend my heartfelt thanks to my beloved siblings, whose memories and shared experiences have enriched this work immeasurably. Thelma, Jerry, Evangeline, Emiliano Jr., Edgar, Francz, Mona and Judith, your recollections and willingness to help recount our family's stories are treasures I hold dear.

A special acknowledgement goes to my sister Mona Liza, who has been an invaluable source of knowledge and meticulous record -keeping. Her dedication to preserving our family's history, documenting dates and events, and meticulously tracking our family tree is a testament to her role as our historian. Her reunion books filled with pictures and stories have been an endless well of inspiration. Her wisdom, invaluable feedback and encouragement have been instrumental in shaping the narrative of this book.

I must also acknowledge my brother Emiliano Jr., whose vivid recollections, particularly those involving our beloved parents, have added a depth and richness to these pages that would have been impossible to achieve without his contribution.

Additionally, I extend my appreciation to my nephew Andrew and my daughter-in-law, Elizabeth, for capturing precious moments on video, which have added a dynamic dimension to my mother's presence within these pages. Watching her speak about her journey from a young girl, to her experience during World War II, and her enduring love story, brought her narrative to life in a way words alone could not. Your recordings have allowed me to relive those cherished memories.

Special thanks to my daughter, Karla and her husband Joseph for their technical expertise and support in converting videos and assisting with research enabling me to incorporate multimedia elements seamlessly into my book.

To Mama's beloved grandchildren, your stories and anecdotes of your precious moments with Lola have added a special dimension to this narrative. Your recollections are cherished keepsakes within these pages.

And finally, to our in-laws, cousins, and friends who knew her, your insights and anecdotes have been instrumental in shaping the narrative of this memoir. Your willingness to share your personal stories of my mother has enhanced the tapestry of memories presented here. My heartfelt special thanks to Amai, my sister-in-law, for your memories and information you shared about my late brother Fred, have added depth and meaning to the pages of my book.

I would like to extend my heartfelt gratitude to Jojo Bersales, the author of the YouTube documentary "Kabilin: The War of Cebu" and the book "The War of Cebu." Jojo's in-depth interview with my mother, capturing her experiences as a courageous member of the Women's Auxiliary Services during the war, has not only preserved her memories but also contributed to the historical documentation of this significant period. Your dedication to preserving the stories of those who lived through the challenging times is deeply appreciated.

I am thankful for the many voices that have contributed to this work, and I hold your stories close to my heart with profound gratitude.

DEDICATION

This book is dedicated to my beloved mother, Monica Babiera Sandalo, whose unwavering love, strength, and resilience continue to inspire me every day. You have been my guiding light and the embodiment of selfless love. Your sacrifices and unwavering support have shaped me into the person I am today.

I also dedicate this book to all the mothers who have faced challenges with courage and grace, nurturing their families with boundless love and dedication. Your sacrifices and tireless efforts are the foundation of our lives, and your love knows no bounds.

To my family, whose support and encouragement have been a a constant source and strength, and to my siblings, who stood by my mother's side and each other through thick and thin. Your unity and solidarity are a testament to the power of family and the bonds that hold us together.

May this book serve as a tribute to the incredible women who have shaped our lives and to the enduring power of faith, love ,resilience, and family.

TABLE OF CONTENT

INTRODUCTION

"I reached the end of the rainbow and found a pot of gold as life's greatest reward for me."

Thank you, Lord! I Praise You! I Love You, by Monica.

Within the pages of this memoir lies the extraordinary story of a woman whose unwavering faith and unyielding strength shaped the very fabric of our lives. My mother, who lived for 97 years, was a remarkable soul who weathered the storms of life with grace, embarked on a journey that defied the odds, and surpassed all expectations.

This memoir is a testament to the unwavering spirit, a celebration of a life lived with purpose and devotion. It is an homage to the countless sacrifices she made, the love she showed us, and the profound impact she had on each and every one of us.

Her journey was not without its share of hardships, but my indomitable mother, she emerged stronger, more resilient, and unbroken in the face of every trial.

With each passing year, she faced a myriad of challenges, yet she stood tall, unwavering in her resolve. In the face of adversity, she summoned the strength of a warrior, finding solace and courage in her unwavering belief and faith in the power of the High Almighty.

Memories and traditions of our family are great treasures. We must not forget what matters most, memory itself or the love that feeds and frames it. Love endures, sparking inspiration and nurturing souls; it possesses the power to reignite. Love thrives in the essence of both the present and the past, while also embracing a boundless future.

As years pass, we become more and more aware of what is important in life. The love and traditions our family shares are priceless and beyond value.

Our memories are gifts we can share by passing on to our children, grandchildren, and generations yet to come.

Mothers hold our hearts forever. Even though the road was hard, my mother endured because a mother's love is linked to her children's hearts. The battle she went through was not chosen, but it must be embraced. In the face of challenges, my mother perseveres, fueled by the hope of providing her children with boundless love, unwavering support, and the precious gift of education and life values. She leaves behind a legacy of strength and courage, inspiring us to thrive independently. I am in awe of her unwavering spirit as she fearlessly conquers all obstacles that come her way.

Through her unwavering dedication, tireless sacrifices, and boundless affection, my mother exemplified the true essence of unconditional love.

Her love transcended the challenges and adversities we faced as a family, becoming the steadfast foundation upon which we built our lives.

In a world that often feels fragmented and disconnected, my mother's story serves as a powerful reminder of the transformative impact of love, compassion, and selflessness. It is my desire that readers, through these pages, will not only gain a deeper appreciation for my mother's remarkable journey but also reflect upon the immeasurable value of familial bonds and the enduring power of love.

My mother's journey is not just a personal narrative. It is a testament to the indomitable spirit and selflessness that resides within mothers all over the world.

May her story serve as a source of inspiration, fostering a greater understanding of the profound impact a mother's love can have on the lives of their children.

Together let us celebrate the beauty of unconditional love and honor the remarkable mothers who have shaped our lives with their unwavering devotion.

As I trace the footsteps of her extraordinary journey, I am filled with awe and gratitude. Her story is one of triumph over adversity, of love's enduring power, and the immeasurable strength of the human spirit. Join me as we delve into the chapters of her life guided by her unwavering faith and fortified by her unwavering love.

CHAPTER 1
ROOTS OF LOVE

"Family: Where life begins, and Love never ends."

As I pen the opening lines of this chapter, I embark on a journey to trace the footsteps of my mother's beginnings. Through the mists of time and memory, I strive to honor her early experiences to capture the essence of the person she was before the weight of responsibility settled upon her shoulders. I find the story of my mother like delicate petals of flowers unfurling under the morning sun; her life unfolded with strength and grace that would shape the lives of twelve children and leave an indelible mark on them.

Born into humble circumstances, my mother emerged from the embrace of a small rural town where dreams often took flight on the wings of hope and determination. It was within this backdrop that her journey of love, resilience, and unwavering devotion began.

As I begin to tell the story of my mother, I am humbled by the sacred connection she shares with the saint who bore her name. In the tapestry of our family's history, my mother, Monica, shines as a radiant thread woven with the blessings of being the youngest of five siblings of 2 boys and 3 girls. Born on the auspicious day of the feast of Santa Monica, she was lovingly bestowed with a name that carried the echoes of a reverend saint.

In the town of Moalboal, the southern part of Cebu province of the Philippines, my mother took her first breath on May 4, 1918. Her full name was Monica Jainar Babiera. She was fondly called Moning. Blessed with the name of the saint, she embodied the virtues of Santa Monica as she navigated the tapestry of her own life.

In the chapters of her life, the influence of Santa Monica's legacy weaves seamlessly with her own story, painting a portrait of a woman who embraces compassion, perseverance, and devotion to her loved ones. As I reflect upon the journey of my dear mother, I am reminded of the profound significance behind her name, which symbolizes the intertwining of faith, love, and family that has shaped her character.

Her parents were Sofia Jainar, born June 11,1887, and Victorio Romano Babiera. Her mother had difficulty during her delivery and almost died, so my mother's birthday celebration was also a thanksgiving for her mother's second life.

Her parents were poor when she was born, but as she was growing up, as she mentioned in her diary, her parents were industrious and hard workers.

In a world where formal education often determines one's path, my mother's parents defied the odds and carved a remarkable story of success. Despite having limited formal education, their unwavering spirit and innate skills propelled them toward a thriving business venture.

My grandfather, a man of humble beginnings, had completed only up to the second grade in his education. While his academic achievements may have been limited, his aptitude for mathematics was unparalleled. Numbers seemed to dance effortlessly in his mind guiding him through complex calculations and enabling him to make financial decisions.

My grandmother, on the other hand, had never received any formal education in reading or writing. Yet her wisdom, intuition, and natural business acumen were exceptional. She possessed an uncanny ability to make money, negotiate deals, and has meaningful connections with suppliers and buyers alike.

Together, armed with their complementary strengths, my grandparents ventured into the world of commerce. Through sheer determination, hard work, and unwavering belief in their abilities, they returned their limited resources into a thriving business enterprise.

In our small town, my grandparent's business ventures extended far beyond the buying of copra (dried coconut meat) and abaca (fiber from a plant called Manila hemp) which is today used for making ropes, twine fishing lines as well as sackcloth. These products were bought from the farmers in different towns and, in turn, sold to big establishments in the city thru their 3 cargo trucks.

The general store they had, which stood tall at the heart of the town, became a hub of activity, drawing locals. Its shelves were adorned with an assortment of goods ranging from daily necessities to rare finds. From fresh produce to household items, my grandparents ensured that their store catered to the diverse needs and desires of the community.

But it was my grandmother's baking skills that made the town look for her freshly baked bread and sweet little Filipino cakes (torta). Then their business expanded to a fishing business. They owned a fishing net and fish pen/ barrier net in the ocean called (bungsud). Through their fishing business, they not only provided sustenance for their own family but also supplied the local markets, ensuring that fresh seafood graced the tables of many households in our town.

Their business was more than just a means of livelihood; they were a source of pride, a testament to their resilience, and a beacon of hope for others pursuing their own entrepreneurial dreams.

While their lack of formal education could have been seen as a disadvantage, my grandparents transformed it into an advantage. They honed their skills through real-life experiences, learning the intricacies of business through trial and error.

This story serves as a reminder that success is not solely determined by academic qualifications but by the willingness to learn, adapt and embrace the opportunities that come our way.

Moalboal has beautiful beaches, and it was in this picturesque setting that my mother's love for swimming was ignited, evoking cherished memories of her childhood. In her recollections, she was a spirited and playful child, and her most treasured possession was a tattered cloth doll, which she fondly mentioned in her diary.

Her parents were very protective and kept her away from other kids, so she didn't have many friends. But she had one close childhood friend named Luisa Gako. They loved playing games like "Hide and Seek" and "Tubiganay," a Filipino outdoor game. These games brought them a lot of joy and made their adventures even more fun.

Her memories of her birthdays were the great celebration of big parties when she was growing up. Her parents celebrated her birthdays, usually with Lechon (roasted pig), chickens, torta (cakes), and many more. As far as my mother remembered, there were a lot of guests during this event.

As my mother's mother had not received any formal education herself, she harbored a deep desire for her daughter to have the educational opportunities she had missed. My grandmother instilled in my mother the importance of studying diligently and excelling in her studies.

Through their guidance, my mother recognized the gift of education as a precious inheritance.

Respecting her parents' hopes for her future, she devoted herself to her studies with unwavering determination. From Grade 1 to 7, she consistently achieved excellent grades, culminating in her graduation as the Salutatorian in Grade 7. Among her preferred subjects were Mathematics, English, and literature, which captivated her intellect and sparked her curiosity. In her leisure time, she found solace and joy in the pages of books, making reading her beloved pastime.

As I reflect on my mother's journey, I am reminded of the incredible gift her parents gave her through their unwavering expectations. Their belief in the power of education and their emphasis on her learning to read and write shaped her into the accomplished individual she is today.

Growing up in a household that embraced Catholic traditions, she witnessed firsthand the significance of honoring and respecting her parents.

She carried this reverence for her parents throughout her life, always striving to show them love, gratitude, and a deep appreciation for the sacrifices they made for her well-being. The guidance and wisdom became her compass in navigating life's challenges and decisions.

The teachings of her faith and the moral compass it provided taught her the importance of obedience and respect towards her parents. Through her example, she showed me the profound impact of having Faith and honoring one's parents can have on shaping a life with love, purpose, and meaning.

From a young age, my mother learned the importance of obedience, heeding her parent's wisdom, and respecting their guidance.

The values she learned from her parents were obedience and spending money wisely, which is one of my mother's legacy to her children. She embedded two qualities she held dear in her children's character: Obedience and thriftiness.

She discovered the power of her mother's love, unconditional support, and steadfast encouragement laid the foundation upon which her own legacy of love would be built.

In her reflections, my mother expressed profound gratitude for these qualities instilled by her parents. Obedience became the compass guiding her choices, leading her towards paths of integrity and self-discipline. It served as a reminder of the importance of honoring commitments. Staying true to one's word and respecting authority.

Thrifty by nature, my mother cultivated a deep appreciation for the value of hard work and the satisfaction of making the most of limited resources. She knew the true worth of each penny saved, and it shaped her ability to navigate the ever-changing tides of life with resilience and foresight.

With gratitude, she recognized that these qualities provided a solid footing in her journey, empowering her to weather storms and embrace opportunities with an unwavering sense of purpose; they serve as guiding principles, lighting her path and reminding her of the values that defined her character.

In the pages that follow, the story unfolds, painted with the colors of resilience, tenderness, and the unyielding power of a mother's love.

CHAPTER 2
EDUCATION AND CAREER

"Education is the passport to the future for tomorrow belongs to those who prepare it today."

-Malcolm X

Join me now, dear reader, as we unravel the chapters that illuminate the intersection of education and career in my mother's extraordinary life.

Each step along her professional path was a testament to her tenacity, resilience, and unwavering excellence.

From the earliest days of her educational journey to the heights she reached in her professional pursuits, she embraced learning as a beacon of empowerment and gateway to her dreams.

She had her elementary school in Moalboal Central School from Grade 1 to Grade 7. Her first schoolhouse was made of wood and galvanized iron roof, and her first teacher was Mr. Alcordo, as she wrote in her diary.

In her elementary school days, her mother prepared everything that was needed in school, and there was no such thing as preschool shopping in those days. She walked to school, which is just a couple of miles from their house, and went home for lunchtime.

Her favorite subjects were arithmetic, science, and English during her elementary school days.

In her early years, she attended elementary school up to Grade 7. After that, she had to move on to high school/college. Although she dreamt of becoming a doctor, her mother encouraged her to choose a teaching career. She pursued her high school studies at Cebu Normal School, which was located 100 kilometers away from her hometown in Cebu City. In her diary, she mentioned that she spent two years there, where high school subjects and teaching methods were combined.

She mentioned that moving away from home made her feel lonely and insecure. According to her, she was lodging in a dormitory called Sto. Rosario, which is run by Catholic Sisters.

She never attended parties of any kind during her college days. Though loneliness may have colored her early college years, it also served her as a catalyst for personal growth and self-discovery.

In those moments of solitude in the dormitory, the weight of newfound responsibilities settled upon her shoulders in her youth as she faced the challenges of adjusting to a new environment yearning for the reassuring presence of her loved ones.

During her high school days, the fashion trend was wearing a uniform and stockings; the uniform had to be 2 inches below the knee. As far as how she dressed herself up as a young adult, she always followed her parents' advice to dress accordingly.

In her high school days, her favorite subjects were English, Mathematics, and Literature. Looking back now, as she claimed, Math and English were of most value to her as she matured in her life. This explains how she continues to perform calculations in her head with astonishing accuracy even in her 90s when many would have relied on external aids.

Her mastery of mathematics shone brightly. From an early age, numbers danced effortlessly in her mind without a calculator or external tools. It was a gift that accompanied her through the chapters of her life, an extraordinary talent that remained sharp as years advanced.

As I explore her letters and diary, I discover that English held a special place in her heart as her favorite subject. But her proficiency in the language wasn't just for herself; she selflessly shared this gift with others. Her words became a beacon of guidance, support, and encouragement for both her family and those who knew her, leaving a lasting impact on their lives

Her eloquence revealed the innermost feelings in her heart.

After her 2 years course at Cebu Normal School, she became a professional teacher at the age of 18 years old. As she wrote in her diary, she enjoyed her job, and she found it very rewarding. She retired after 42 years of her career at the age of 60.

Throughout her life, my mother cherished the wisdom and guidance passed down from her own mother -a beacon of strength and a source of unwavering support. It was her mother who, in gentle words and a knowing smile, imparted the advice that would shape my mother's path. "Teaching is a noble calling, my child," as what her mother told her. As she encouraged her to pursue teaching, she also mentioned its affordability financially and earning her degree in 2 years as well.

In spite of her dream to be a doctor, she heeded her mother's counsel and pursued a career in teaching, devoting herself to the education and growth of young minds. And as the years unfolded, she discovered the truth in her mother's words-teaching was indeed a noble calling, a vocation. Pouring her heart and soul into her role as an educator, she discovered that teaching was the most fulfilling and rewarding profession for her.

She got her teaching job at Moalboal Elementary School. For the first 2 years, she taught a Grade 2 class and then moved to a Grade 4 class in the same elementary school. During her adulthood, she lived with her parents.

Within the walls of her classroom, my mother held the reputation of a strict disciplinarian-a formidable presence that commanded respect and demanded order. Her students, and even we, her own children, knew that misbehavior would not go unnoticed or punished. Yet, behind her firm exterior, there lay a deep well of love and an unwavering commitment to instilling discipline and shaping character.

One defining aspect of her disciplinary approach was her signature pinching method. It was not an act of abuse or cruelty but rather a means to drive home the importance of obedience and accountability. With a gentle yet firm pinch, she would remind us of the boundaries we were expected to uphold and the consequences that awaited those who strayed.

Looking back, I can see the lasting impact of her disciplinary approach. The students, now adults themselves, often recall the lessons learned within her classroom-the pinches that serve as gentle nudges toward personal growth and self-improvement. They remember her as a figure of authority but also as someone who genuinely cared about their well-being.

In recounting the story of my mother's teaching career, there is a chapter that stands as a testament to her unwavering integrity and commitment to fairness.

For my mother, being both a mother and a teacher meant upholding a higher standard-a standard that demands transparency, equality, and prioritization of the greater good. She recognized that awarding my sister Mona Liza the first honors, even if she deserves it, could be perceived as nepotism and undermine the integrity of the entire academic institution.

It was a painful decision to make, as it meant momentarily disappointing her own daughter. But she understood that in doing so, she was teaching us a profound lesson of fairness and integrity.

During her teaching career, there was a contest among teachers of a district comprising several towns for the title "Most Popular Lady of 1936, Moalboal Cebu" She was 18 years old then when she won the title and recognition and honor that she held for two consecutive years.

Miss Monica Babiera
Most Popular Lady of 1936
Toalbool C.R.,

Her popularity was not derived from a desire for attention or self-promotion but rather from the authentic connections she forged with those around her. Her extraordinary gift lay in making people feel seen, heard, and deeply valued. This was a testament not only to her personal charisma but also to the profound impact she had on the lives of those around her.

In celebrating my mother's teaching career, I pay homage to the profound influence of maternal wisdom and the power of a chosen path. It is a testament to the enduring bond between generations, where love, guidance, and the pursuit of purpose intertwine, having lives leaving a lasting legacy. In retrospect, my mother came to understand that her parents' expectations went beyond mere academic success; they were grounded in a profound sense of love and care. Belief in her potential. Their unwavering commitment to her education became a catalyst for her personal growth and a testament to their unconditional love and support.

CHAPTER 3
LOVE AND MARRIAGE

"Love one another, but make not a bond of love: Let it rather be a moving sea between the shores of your souls."

-Khalil Gibran

Love has a mysterious way of finding its path, defying all obstacles, and triumphing over adversity. Such was the case of my parents, whose love story unfolded through a series of handwritten letters and the daring persistence of a young man who refused to let societal norms stand in the way of his affection.

As I was reading her diary and reviewing the recorded interview with a family member, her love story is a reminder that love knows no boundaries, even in the face of adversity.

It all began on a town fiesta, a hometown celebration in honor of the Moalboal's Patron Saint San Juan Nepumoceno. My father, Emiliano Quinones Sandalo, a talented basketball player from Silliman University, was one of the players in the game tournament. My mother was introduced to him by a friend. Although their encounter was brief, it sparked a flame that would burn brightly across the pages of their love story.

My mother was 19 years old when she met my father, and she described my father as handsome, strong, and soft-spoken. He was a friend of my mother's brother, and worked for him for a while.

In an era before instant messages and digital communication, they turned to a timeless form of expression - the love letter. Each letter was a treasure, hand delivered by loyal friends who understood the depth of their affection and the significance of their words.

However, the road to their union was not an easy one. My mother's parents were known for their strictness and protective nature, shielding their daughter from the world outside their home. Male friendships were discouraged, and the prospect seemed like an unattainable dream, but love knows no boundaries.

My mother's parents showered her with material possessions, a Chevrolet car, and a grand piano, attempts to sway her heart and distract her from her longing for marriage, but they were no match for the indomitable spirit of love that burned within her. While the gifts were appreciated, they could never replace the deep connection she had forged with the man who had captured her heart.

In the end, her parents had no choice but to accept her decision. They saw that their daughter's happiness lay not in material possessions but in the arms of the man she loved.

In the heart of our small town, my father orchestrated a traditional Filipino courtship called "Harana", serenading my mother with a group of musicians armed with musical instruments gathered in front of her house. The music flowed through the night, melodic tunes wrapped around my mother's home, a tribute of love and devotion that blossomed between them.

My parents had their own love song entitled "It's A Sin to Tell a Lie," a song in 1936 by Billy Mayhew.

In telling this chapter of my parent's love story, I am reminded of the profound impact of our cultural traditions, the way they intertwine with our personal narratives and the lasting memories they create.

After exchanging love letters in secret for 3 long years, my father sent a proposal letter twice, which was sent with anticipation but was met with silence from my mother's parents.

Undeterred by the silence, my father resolved to take matters into his own hands. With unwavering determination and a heart filled with love, he made an unannounced visit to my mother's home, seeking an audience with her parents. It was a bold move, driven by love that refused to be silent and a commitment that defied all odds.

As he stood before them earnestly, he expressed his intentions, his devotion to their daughter, and his unwavering commitment to building a life together. His sincerity, paired with an undeniable connection that has blossomed between my parents, proved to be an irresistible force. And so, with hesitant nods and flickers of acceptance, my mother's parents granted their blessing and asked my father to come back with his parents to meet with them to discuss the wedding plans.

Having been raised in the Protestant faith, my father cultivated a deep connection to his religious beliefs. But as he embarked on the path of marrying my mother, he faced a crossroads where love and faith intersected. With each step toward conversion, my father embraced the rich tapestry of Catholic traditions, rituals, and sacraments.

In embracing Catholicism, my father not only honored my mother's heritage but also laid the foundation of our family's spiritual journey. It was an act of selflessness, symbolizing the depths of his commitment and the length he was willing to go ensure that their union was blessed within the faith that held such meaning to my mother.

Their grand wedding on June 3, 1939, was not merely an event but a transformative experience that forever altered the course of their lives. In her diary, my mother described their wedding as the happiest moment of their lives. As I reflect upon their grand wedding, I am reminded of the profound impact of love and the power of a day that becomes a cherished milestone in their story.

She described her wedding dress as a long gown, white lace, full of sequence decorations with a long tail veil which the wedding picture said all.

My father, who was so handsome on their memorable day, wore a white suit and white pants.

Relatives and friends were all happy to help with the decorations, and as she said in her diary, food was abundant, and flowers were taken care of by her friends.

Their wedding was a simple affair, not adorned with extravagant flowers, but abundant with delectable food. On the special day, they rode in a car adorned with flowers. However, there was no honeymoon planned after the wedding.

She described my fathers as being loving, thoughtful, and industrious. My father's hobbies were playing chess and playing billiards. Sometimes they go to friends' parties together. They had a busy life after they got married. It was their parent's request for them to live with them after marriage. My mother's parents wanted my father to learn the family business.

Living with my grandparents allowed my parents to witness the sacrifice and hard work that went into building and sustaining a successful family business. It instilled in them a deep appreciation for the legacy they were inheriting, and the guidance they received was not limited to the business realm; it extended to life lessons, personal growth, and the importance of nurturing strong family ties.

The birth of their first child brought immeasurable joy and a renewed sense of purpose to my parents' lives. It was a moment of overwhelming love and responsibility as they held their precious bundle of joy. As she wrote in her diary, they experienced both excitement and fear. They named their first child Thelma Expedita, and she was born on April 19, 1940. They marveled at the miracle of life and embraced the challenges and joys that came with parenthood.

Then a second child came. His name was Leo, and he was born on March 2, 1941. However, their joy was overshadowed by fear and uncertainty as the news reached their ears of the invasion of the Japanese in the Philippines during World War 11 on December 8. 1941, starting in Bataan.

With two young children to care for and a third baby on the way, my parents along with my grandparents faced a tough decision. They chose to evacuate to the mountains in search of safety from the turmoil of war. When the Fall of Cebu occurred, with the Japanese invasion on April 10, 1942, the entire town of Moalboal evacuated, seeking refuge and hiding from the invading forces.

It was a time of upheaval and sacrifices as they left behind their home, possessions, and familiar comforts of their lives. They just had enough food for them that just could last for a few months. They embraced the unknown, driven by a deep instinct to protect their children and secure their future.

In the pages of their memoir, my parents recount the mix of emotions they experienced during this time - the fear of uncertainty but also the profound love and resilience that sustained them.

CHAPTER 4
LIFE DURING WORLD WAR II

"Though war may darken our days, it is in the depths of adversity that our true strength emerges, illuminating the path to hope and resilience."

On December 8, 1941, the Japanese attacked the Commonwealth of the Philippines. The combined Filipino-American army was defeated in the Battle of Bataan., but guerrilla resistance against the Japanese continued throughout the war.

The Japanese forces invaded Cebu and occupied the city, establishing control over the region. They imposed strict rules and regulations, including curfews, forced labor, and restriction on movements and communications.

Regardless of their occupations, some Filipinos bravely resisted Japanese control through the formation of guerrilla movements and underground organizations. Their main objective was to challenge Japanese authority, and they engaged in acts of sabotage, intelligence gathering, and offering support to the Allied forces."

The Japanese occupation was marked by numerous massacres and atrocities committed against the Filipino population.

The war brought economic hardship to the Filipino people. Cebu experienced significant damage and destruction during the war. Infrastructure, buildings, and homes were destroyed or damaged by bombings and military operations.

The impact of the Japanese War on the lives of Filipinos, including Cebu, was profound. As the battle unfolded, civilians faced great hardship and danger. Many Filipinos were forced to evacuate their homes and seek shelter in safer areas, such as the mountains or neighboring islands.

The Japanese occupation had already brought significant suffering to the people in Cebu, with the locals enduring various forms of oppression and brutality.

As World War II progressed, a group of Japanese soldiers arrived by boat and invaded my parent's hometown, Moalboal. At this time, as the ravages of war swept across our town, my parents, along with her parents, found themselves thrust into a world of uncertainty and upheaval.

With the mounting threats and dangers of World War II, they made a difficult decision to seek refuge in the mountains.

The journey to the mountains was arduous, filled with hardships and challenges. But amidst the hardship, they found strength in each other and in the unwavering love they held for their children. Their determination and resilience became a guiding light, illuminating the path ahead even in the darkest times.

In the mountains, they found a place in between two hills, and they created a makeshift home, relying on their resourcefulness and the support of fellow evacuees. It was a time of bonding and community as they forged connections with others who were also seeking safety and solace amidst the chaos of war. Together they found a support system, offering comfort, aid, and a sense of unity in the face of adversity.

Life in the mountains demanded resilience, resourcefulness, and adaptability. When their food supply was running out, they had a barter system with the farmers. Their extra clothing in exchange for root crops like sweet potato, rice, eggs, and any edible products on the farm. The routine of daily work took a new meaning as they sought stability amidst the ever-changing tides of war.

But amidst the hardship and sacrifices, there was a moment of joy when my sister was delivered on December 23, 1942, in a little hut in the mountains. They named her Jeremiah Luz. Even in the midst of war, they found solace in each other and discovered that the indomitable spirit of the human heart could not be extinguished.

For almost three years, their lives unfolded amidst the rugged beauty of the mountainous terrain, far removed from the comforts and familiarity of their former existence. They found solace and forged a new way of life, driven by an unwavering determination to protect their family and preserve their hope in the face of adversity.

When they were in the mountains, my mother remembered the sounds of the bombing. Then when they heard planes up in the air, forming the word USA in the clouds, they were relieved and shouting with joy clapping their hands. Finally, they found hope and could start their normal life.

The war ended on September 2, 1945, when US General Douglas MacArthur accepted Japan's formal surrender.

The next chapter will be about my mother's dedication, strength, and selflessness in balancing her responsibilities as a mother and her active participation in the guerrilla movement.

CHAPTER 5
WOMEN'S AUXILIARY SERVICE: BALANCING DUTY AND MOTHERHOOD

In the midst of the tumultuous times during the war, my mother, Monica, stood as a pillar of strength, embodying the pirate of resilience and service. She not only cared for her children in the mountains but also played a vital role in the Women's Auxiliary Service, a group of courageous women who provided invaluable support to the guerrilla forces. Her unwavering commitment to the cause and her ability to juggle the demands of motherhood and activism made her an extraordinary figure in the midst of chaos.

In the documentary on the war of Cebu, titled "Kabilin: The Fall of Cebu" by Jojo Bersales (Part of a series of documentaries of World War II as seen on YouTube), my mother was interviewed personally by the author as she was one of the living women at war.

My mother's voice resonated as she recounted her experiences as a member of the Women's Auxiliary Service. She vividly described the challenges they faced, from sourcing scarce food and clothing to ensuring the well-being of the fighters. Despite the constant dangers and hardships, my mother and the other women persevered, driven by a deep sense of duty and a desire to contribute to the fight for freedom.

Being mentioned in "The War of Cebu," a documentary book, serves as a testament to my mother's significance in the guerrilla movement.

This book describes the entire Japanese invasion and occupation of Cebu up to the pre-liberation bombings by the American forces in late 1944 and the fateful Japanese surrender on August 28. 1945.

The book chronicled the heroic acts of individuals like my mother, capturing the sacrifices and contributions for future generations to remember. It was a proud moment for our family to see her name acknowledged, a tribute to her unwavering commitment to the cause.

Here is the excerpt from the section of the book: "Women in War."

"Monica was already a 21-year-old teacher when the Japanese finally arrived in Moalboal. She joined the Women's Auxiliary Service, supplying food and other sundries to the southern Cebu Forces."

Monica has survived the war and continues to live in her post-war residence at the center of Moalboal. Except for the church, convent, and elementary school, no pre-war houses can be found in town because Moalboal was burned to the ground by the Japanese in retaliation for the successful ambush of Japanese troops at the historic "Battle of Tomonoy" in 1944. Tomonoy is a little barrio which is located in Moalboal. My mother received a certificate for her service.

Through her involvement in the Women's Auxiliary Service and her mention in "The War of Cebu", my mother's story became intertwined with the larger narrative of resilience and resistance during the war. Her dedication, strength, and ability to balance the demands of motherhood and her duty to the cause exemplify the extraordinary women who stood tall amidst the chaos; my mother's legacy as a member of the Women's Auxiliary Service will forever inspire us, reminding us the power of selflessness, courage and the indomitable spirit of those who fought for freedom.

CHAPTER 6
BUILDING LOVE, STRENGTH AND 12 HEARTS: OUR HOME AFTER WORLD WAR 11

"NURTURING A FAMILY'S JOURNEY"

"Home is where our story begins, where love resides and where memories reside"-Unknown.

Section 1: Our Home
Rebuilding Amidst the Ashes

A new beginning. In the aftermath of the war, as the smoke cleared and the scar of the conflict started to heal, my parents stood amidst the ruins of the once-vibrant town.

The Japanese had taken its toll leaving behind a trail of destruction, including the loss of their family home. But in the face of adversity, they were determined to rebuild not only their physical dwelling but also the foundation of their growing family.

No longer living under the shelter of their parent's roof, they embraced the opportunity to forge their own path, laying the groundwork for a future filled with love, dreams and the arrival of nine precious children.

And so, with hope in their hearts and a vision of a brighter future, my parents began the arduous task of rebuilding their home and laying the foundations of a life filled with love, laughter and the echoes of their children's footsteps.

My parents were busy working after the war. As my mother continued to pursue her professional career in teaching, my father's entrepreneurial spirit soared to new heights.

Section 2: The Entrepreneurial Spirit: A Legacy of Success

After the war, when everything was being fixed up, my father's strong desire to start and run businesses grew even more, leaving an indelible mark on the community and our family legacy. With determination and a keen eye for opportunity, he embarked on a journey that would transform his humble beginnings into a thriving business empire.

At the heart of my father's ventures was his booming trucking business which became a lifeblood of the local construction industry. With his trucks, he transported essential building materials like sand and gravel, fueling the rapid growth of housing projects in the region. His truck became a familiar sight on the roads, symbolizing progress and the promise of a brighter future. He managed to add passenger trucking as his business expanded.

In addition to the trucking business, my father's business extended to a thriving buy-and-sell. His buy and sell business extended thru traveling in different cities.

He had an uncanny ability to spot opportunities and seize them with calculated precision.

Our house was a vibrant place that buzzed with activity and served as a hub for our family's diverse ventures. On the ground floor, there was a grand variety store where my father offered a wide range of products to the townspeople. Adjacent to it was the buying and weighing station for Copra, a vital component of our family's successful buy and sell.

Amidst the busy commerce, we had a special section dedicated to my father's passion for rooster raising and cockfighting. The roosters were cared for with utmost attention and love, reflecting my father's dedication to his interests beyond business.

The booming trucking business and the thriving buy-and-sell enterprise were more than just a means of financial prosperity. They were a testament to my father's vision, courage, and unwavering belief in the power of hard work. His business not only provided for our family but also became the pillar of the community, a testament to the transformative power of entrepreneurship.

The legacy of my father's businesses lives on, woven into the fabric of our family's history; they serve as a reminder of his ingenuity, resilience and the endless possibilities that exist when passion meets opportunity.

Section 3: The Joy of an Ever-Growing family

As the years unfolded, their hearts opened wider, welcoming new lives into their embrace. With each new arrival, the sparkle in their eyes grew brighter, and their smiles stretched a little wider. They cherished the unique gifts and personalities that each child brought into their lives, celebrating the beautiful tapestry of their diverse personalities.

It was as if their love had an infinite capacity to multiply, blossoming with each new addition to our family. They reveled in the chaos of a household bustling with the energy of twelve children, cherishing every moment spent together. From the late-night lullabies to the laughter echoing through the halls, they found solace and fulfillment in the warmth of our united hearts.

Their love was a testament to the power of selflessness, sacrifice, and unconditional devotion. They poured their hearts into nurturing and guiding us, teaching us the values of compassion, resilience and the importance of family. They navigated the challenges and triumphs of raising twelve children with grace and unwavering love, leaving an indelible mark on each of our lives.

Section 4: Blessed Deliverance

A Mother's Journey of 12 Healthy Births

Within the tapestry of my mother's life, there exists an extraordinary chapter filled with the miraculous gift of birth. Against all odds and superstition, she traversed the path of motherhood, bringing forth twelve beautiful souls into the world. This section unveils the remarkable tale of her unwavering strength, resilience and divine blessings that ensured each delivery was a testament to her health and the well-being of her precious babies.

The home births, while unconventional by modern standards, fostered an environment of intimacy and familiarity. Our family home became the sacred space where new life unfolded. Where the echoes of newborn cries intertwined with love and warmth that enveloped us all.

Through twelve pregnancies, my mother navigated the sacred path of motherhood with astonishing grace. The births of her children became a testament to her incredible strength as she faced labor and delivery with fortitude and unwavering trust in the miracle of life. The midwife, a steadfast companion on this sacred journey, provided guidance and care, ensuring the safety and well-being of both the mother and child.

As we celebrate the miracle of life and the enduring bond that unites our family, we honor the remarkable journey of my mother, a woman who embraced the sacred dance of child birth with grace, resilience and an unwavering love that transcends all boundaries. Her experience of delivering 11 children at home remains a cherished chapter a testament of the power of natural birth. This remains a cherished chapter in our family's history, a testament to the power of natural birth and the indomitable spirit of motherhood.

With each successful home birth, our family's love and gratitude deepened as we marveled at the strength and fortitude displayed by our beloved matriarch.

Today, as I reflect on the journey of my mother's twelve deliveries, I am filled with awe and profound gratitude for the divine protection and guidance that surrounded my mother and her twelve pregnancies. This is an awe- inspiring story of my mother's unwavering love, resilience, and the remarkable blessings that graced our family.

Section 5: Breaking the Superstition

Embracing the Blessing of 12 Children

Within the tapestry of our family's history, there lies a curious thread of superstition passed down through generations and woven into the fabric of our cultural beliefs. An aged -old tale whispered in hushed voices, it tells us a perceived imbalance, an ominous omen associated with families blessed with 12 children, divided evenly between sons and daughters. However, within the narratives of our lives, we challenge this belief and redefine it as a blessing rather than a curse.

To counteract this perceived ill fortune, our family embraced a unique and seemingly extraordinary practice. With great solemnity and unwavering determination to safeguard our parents' well-being, we gathered together for a sit-down dinner meticulously arranged by a non-relative. This curious ritual, an attempt to ward off the dark cloud of superstition, became an inedible part of our family's story.

Section 6: Our Humble Abode

Our Home: A Sanctuary of Love and Memories

Our family's big house stood as a symbol of togetherness and resilience and shared experiences that molded us into the individuals we are today. Nestled amidst the bustling streets, it provided a sanctuary where laughter echoed through its walls, where dreams were nurtured and bonds of sibling hood grew stronger with each passing day.

With four bedrooms accommodating the twelve of us plus my parents, our living arrangements were as lively as they were cozy. Space may have been limited, but the love and sense of camaraderie within those walls knew no bounds.

Within the walls of our family home, a unique arrangement unfolded each night. This section delves into the enchanting evening when the younger children found solace on the wooden floor of our large living room, accompanied by the soft embrace of a woven mat (called "Banig", a traditional handwoven mat made of buri (palm) or pandamus or reed leaves), while the adults sought rest in the cozy confines of their rooms. It was during these nights that the melodies of piano keys played by my big sisters and grandmother on my father's side echoed through the house, weaving a tapestry of love, music and togetherness.

Each evening as the younger children found their designated spots on the wooden floor of the living room, the walls echoed with the harmonious symphony of siblings' laughter, playful banter, and occasional bickering, creating a symphony of life that resonated through every nook and cranny. As a family, we cherished the feelings of togetherness and unity that were fostered through this unique sleeping arrangement, which had a lasting impact on our appreciation for music, togetherness, and the power of creating a harmonious home.

In the embrace of woven mats and the echoes of piano melodies, our family found solace and closeness.

Our house, a time capsule of a bygone era, held treasures that modern conveniences could never replicate. One solitary toilet, a luxury we all started, serves as a testament to our ability to adapt and make do with the resources at hand. With a touch of creativity and a sprinkle of patience, we learned the art of coordination and timing, ensuring that everyone's needs were met even in the face of limited facilities.

In a world where televisions were yet to dominate the living room, our entertainment came in the form of radio waves that filled the air with enchanting melodies and captivating stories.

As the sun dipped below the horizon, casting its golden glow on the streets outside, we traded the flicker of electric lights for the gentle glow of Petromax and gas lamps. These humble sources of illumination gave our home a warm nostalgic radiance.

While our surroundings may have lacked the modern conveniences of today, our playtime was an adventure in itself. With the big buses rumbling past our doorstep, we turned the untamed streets into our playground, fueling our imagination with the rush of passing vehicles and the spirited laughter that filled the air. It was a time of carefree exploration, where creativity flourished against the backdrop of a somewhat unsafe but thrilling environment.

Looking back, those humble living conditions hold a special place in our hearts. They taught us the value of simplicity, resourcefulness and the joy that can be found in the company of loved ones. Our house may have lacked the trappings of modernity, but it overflowed with the intangible treasures of love, laughter and shared experiences. It served as a constant reminder that true happiness is not found in material possessions but in the warmth of relationships and the cherished memories that we hold dear.

As we journey through life, we carry the lessons learned in that humble abode with us. It shaped our resilience, instilled in us an appreciation for the simple joys, and fostered an unbreakable bond that transcends time and distance. Our big house may have been filled with laughter, chaos, and the occasional challenge, yet, it stands as proof of our family's love's resilience and the lasting force of home.

Section 7: A Foundation of Respect and Obedience

Nurturing Values through Discipline

This section delves into the pivotal role of discipline in shaping the values of respect and obedience within our family. It explores the unwavering commitment of our parents to instill these core principles in their children, creating these values through their own actions and behaviors.

Within the walls of our home, a culture of respect and obedience flourished, fostered by the unwavering discipline of our parents.

Through their firm but loving guidance, our parents imparted the importance of respect for authorities, adherence to rules and the understanding that obedience is not merely compliance but an expression of love and trust.

In the realm of our childhood, a tapestry of love and discipline was woven with great care. Within the walls of our home, rules were established, and expectations were set. Our parents believed that the path to a fulfilling and successful life required a strong foundation built on respect and obedience. Misbehavior was not taken lightly, as they recognized that the choices we made in our youth would shape the adults we would become.

When someone among us transgressed, be it through lies or actions contrary to the principles of our households, collective accountability was upheld. It was not a matter of singling out the individual but rather a reminder that our actions held consequences for the entire family. The communal sense of responsibility fostered a bond of support and understanding among siblings, reinforcing the values we were taught.

The tools of discipline were at times formidable, yet they were wielded with purpose.

My father's whip and my mother's pinches carried weight, serving as physical reminders of the importance of obedience and the repercussions of our choices.

While they caused temporary discomfort, their intention was never to inflict lasting harm but rather to drive home the lessons we needed to learn.

Through the lens of time and reflection, I understand that their approach was rooted in love and a sense of responsibility as parents. Their discipline was not an act of abuse but rather a steadfast commitment to our growth and character development.

Anecdote: The Close Call

A Harrowing incident, Lessons in Responsibility and Sibling Bond.

Within the fabric of our family's memories, there exists an incident that forever serves as a reminder of the importance of vigilance and responsibility. This particular anecdote, etched in our collective consciousness, shed light on a moment when our youngest sister Judith Leila around 3 years old at that time, narrowly escaped a devastating accident. It is a tale of both regret and resilience, highlighting the bonds of sibling hood and the valuable lessons we learned as a result.

It was a carefree afternoon when most of us younger siblings were playing on the street in front of our house when my younger sister, mcre three years old at that time, ventured out of the busy street when a bus came dangerously close to her and stopped just an inch away. The heart-stopping moment when my sister's life hung in the balance and the collectively tense seconds felt like an eternity culminating in a collective sigh of relief as she was swiftly pulled out of harm's way. We panicked and raced to intervene. The vivid picture of her inch away from the bus was so terrifying that I did not even notice who pulled her out of danger. Then a moment of realization when the gravity of the situation hit home, and my siblings and I realized that we had neglected the duty of looking after our younger sister.

When our parents learned about the incident, we were calmly asked who was responsible for my younger sister's near tragedy. Since all of us were responsible for watching over her we kept our silence. All of us received disciplinary action, and conversations took place on the lessons learned from the near tragedy, emphasizing the importance of vigilance, responsibility and the realization that the safety and well-being of each family member were shared responsibilities.

The close call that day left an indelible mark on our family's collective memory, a constant reminder of the importance of vigilance, accountability and sibling unity.

In this section, we have explored the profound influence of our parents' discipline in fostering a culture of respect and obedience within our family. Their unwavering commitment to instilling these values has left an indelible mark on each of us, shaping the individuals we have become. As we continue our journey, we carry with us the lessons we learned from their guidance, knowing that the values of respect and obedience will continue to guide us throughout our lives.

Section 8: The Whistle and Family Time

"The Whistle's Call: Gathering as One"

Standing at the window with a commanding presence and a knowing smile, our father would emit a unique and commanding whistle that carried both authority and love. It was the sound that echoed with a powerful message, transcending the distance between us and conveying a simple yet unyielding expectation: be home by 6pm.

The consequence of being late was not to be taken lightly, for our father's whistle was a reminder of accountability and the importance of following through on our commitments.

The whistle was more than just a call to gather for dinner. It symbolized the values of discipline, punctuality and responsibility that our father held dear. It was his way of teaching us the importance of honoring commitments, respecting the time and efforts of others and of instilling a sense of structure and order in our lives.

To this day, the memory of that whistle lingers as a gentle call that reminds us of the lesson learned, the structure instilled and the unwavering love that guided our father's actions.

That simple yet powerful whistle was more than just a means of summoning us home. It was a testament to our father's unwavering commitment to our well-being, his steadfast presence in our lives and the lasting impact of his guidance and love.

Section 9: Prayer and Gratitude

In the heart of our family rituals, there was a simple yet profound tradition that unfolded before every meal. It was a moment when our father, with a gentle yet firm voice, would ask us to pause in prayer. It was a practice that went beyond the physical act of nourishing our bodies: it was a reminder to nourish our souls and express gratitude for the blessings bestowed upon us.

In those moments of prayer, we learned to express gratitude, not only for the food before us but for the love that surrounded us, the opportunities that awaited us and the strength that guided us. It taught us to pause, even for just a brief moment, to recognize the blessings in our lives and to offer thanks for the abundance we were fortunate to receive.

Through the act of saying grace, our father taught us to appreciate the nourishment before, not just as physical sustenance, but as a symbol of the love and care that went into every meal. It was a reminder that our food was a gift, a manifestation of the earth's abundance and the efforts of those who labored to bring it to our table.

Section 10: The Family Support

Embracing our Extended Family

In our family, the love and support we received extended beyond the boundaries of our immediate household. Our extended family and community played an essential role in creating a nurturing environment for all of us, especially during times when our parents were working. One of the remarkable ways in which this support manifested was through the dedicated efforts of our extended family members, who stepped in as caregivers. These individuals, often less fortunate themselves, embraced their role with open hearts, providing us with love, care, and a sense of belonging when our parents were away. Their selflessness and devotion made a profound impact on our upbringing, fostering a deep appreciation for the strength of our family bonds and the power of community.

A special tribute to Sebastiana Paquera, as a caregiver, this family member had been an anchor in our lives. She had stood by our side, offering steadfast and unwavering support. From the time my mother was a young child, this remarkable individual stepped in as a caregiver and provided not only physical care but also emotional support during times of joy and adversity. As the years passed and my grandparents passed away, this family member remained a pillar of strength, choosing to stay with our family and continue the legacy of care and devotion that has been established. The bond between her and our family is built on a foundation of unwavering loyalty and trust.

This remarkable individual's role as family support extends beyond her immediate caregiving duties. She had been a bridge between generations, ensuring that our family's traditions, values and stories were passed down and cherished.

In conclusion, we express our gratitude for the discipline of our parents and the role it placed in shaping and preparing us for the challenges of the world.

Our parent's unconditional love for their twelve children has a profound impact on our family. Their nurturing spirit, unwavering dedication, and firm but loving discipline have shaped each of us individuals we are today. We are deeply in gratitude for the sacrifices our parents made and the values they instilled in us.

A comparison of the old house then and now

CHAPTER 7
12 SIBLINGS, 12 PERSONALITIES: A KALEIDOSCOPE OF ONE FAMILY

"Families are like branches on a tree. We grow in different directions, yet our roots remain as one" -Anonymous.

Twelve Hearts, Twelve Souls, each unique in their own way, together weaving the tapestry of our family's history.

As our family continued to grow, each new addition brought its own special joy and blessing. From my older and younger siblings, I witnessed the wonders of new life and the beauty of their individual personalities.

In the tapestry of our family, each thread represented a distinct personality, a vibrant hue that contributed to the rich mosaic of our lives. As one of the twelve children, I marveled at the kaleidoscope of individuality that unfolded within the walls of our home. From the boisterous laughter of the extroverts to the quiet introspection of the introverts, each of us brought a unique spirit that added color and depth to our family tapestry.

In our home, love flowed freely, abundant and unyielding. It was love that recognized and embraced the essence of each child, nurturing our growth and fostering our individuality. Our parents, with their extraordinary ability to navigate the intricacies of our personalities, created a tapestry of love where all twelve threads were equally cherished and celebrated.

As the middle child, occupying the space between the older and younger siblings, I discovered a distinct vantage point from which to observe and navigate the ever-evolving dynamics of our family, sandwiched between the responsibilities of the older siblings and the adorations bestowed upon the youngest, I found my own place, a role that would shape my journey within the tapestry of our lives.

In my own unique experience and observations, here are my siblings, from oldest to youngest, with their own unique gifts and personalities that each one brought to our lives.

First Family Reunion

Dec 25 1963

1. Thelma —From the Court to the Tiles: A Sister's Dual Passions. A Trailblazer Senior (April 19, 1940)

Thelma, the oldest among us, possesses a captivating tomboyish spirit that has never faded with time. Fearlessly independent and fiercely protective of her own space, she navigates life with a steadfast determination to minimize stress and chaos. With a penchant for self-preservation, she prefers to focus on herself, cherishing moments of tranquility that allow her to recharge and find solace.

Among the twelve siblings, my sister Thelma stands out as the embodiment of an unwavering passion for sports and camaraderie. As the sun rises each day, she laces up her tennis shoes and hits the court, a flurry of energy and focus.

Her love for tennis has been a constant source of joy and fulfillment for her. Her determination to stay active and fit has contributed to her overall vitality and longevity.

Her passion for tennis, remarkable stamina and dedication to the sport at 83 is remarkable.

But it is not just tennis that captivates her heart; the world of Mahjong holds a special place in her daily routine. Like clockwork, she gathers her group of cherished friends at her home, where laughter and tiles clacking become a symphony of connection and joy. For at least four hours every day, they indulge in spirited games, their passion for Mahjong binding them like a tight-knit family.

In her world, the lines between competition and companionship blur, and it's not about winning or losing -it's about the journey of connecting with others through shared passions. Her unwavering dedication to both tennis and Mahjong serves as an inspiration to us all, reminding us to find joy in the simple pleasures of life and the company of kindred spirits.

Apart from her dual passions, she is also a silent academic sponsor to one of the nieces in the family, supporting her education financially.

2. Leo— The Quiet and Intellectual. (March 2, 1941 - July 11, 2020)

His gentle demeanor and sharp intellect were a beacon of quiet wisdom in our family. His passion for books was unmatched, as he delved into the carefully woven words of various authors from around the world. Preferring the company of written narratives over the noise of everyday life, he found solace and inspiration in the pages that transport him to realms both known and unknown. He was a true bookworm with an insatiable thirst for knowledge.

He had a knack for dry humor that often caught us off guard, leaving us in stitches with a smile on our faces. Not just a man of words, Leo was also a handyman ready to tackle a project with ease. His brilliant mind was an invaluable asset to our family. Beyond his professional accomplishment, he was a devoted husband, father and grandfather cherishing the bonds of family with a love that knew no bounds.

He can surprise you by singing and dancing during unexpected moments. Though quiet in nature, his actions spoke volumes, leaving an enduring legacy of compassion, strength and perseverance. In the memories we hold dear and the lives he touched, his spirit lives on, a cherished cornerstone in the foundation of our family's journey.

3. Jeremiah — The Nurturing Soul/ SacrificingAbroad - (December 13, 1942)

Beneath her infectious liveliness lies a heart that is incredibly sensitive with a nurturing and thoughtful soul. A remarkable sister, a true embodiment of determination and sacrifice. With unwavering dedication, she ventured into the unknown, working abroad to provide a better future for her family. Despite the geographical distance, her love and support knew no bounds, as she managed to raise her children with an iron will and nurturing heart.

While her journey was challenging, her resilience was boundless. She embraced her role as a mother guiding and nurturing her children to achieve greatness. Through her hard work and determination, she paved the way for them to pursue their dreams and become accomplished professionals, a testament to her enduring love and selfless sacrifice.

We witness the legacy of her dedication as her children and their own children thrive, each carrying forward her values and spirit. She may have been far from home, but her presence and impact were felt in every milestone and achievement of her family.

Her nurturing nature seeks not only to provide care and support but also to foster a sense of reciprocity and appreciation. Her sensitivity embodies the essence of family-oriented love and devotion. She continues to pour her love and care into those around her, knowing that her nurturing effort has the potential to create a profound connection and foster a sense of unity.

Beyond her nurturing soul and sacrifices for her family, so is our family's trusted treasurer. She is responsible and reliable when it comes to handling money and financial matters during collective activities. Her honesty and trustworthiness make her an essential figure in managing finances in the family.

4. Evangeline. - Outspoken Advocate /Adventurous Wanderer. (January 22, 1945)

She possesses a unique blend of charisma and conviction, unafraid to voice her opinions and advocate for what she believes in. While her assertiveness can, at times, be overwhelming, her passion and unwavering dedication to her convictions are admirable. She stands as a reminder that diversity of thought is essential for growth and understanding within a family.

Despite facing physical limitations, she possesses an unparalleled love for travel and a deep desire to immerse in new experiences. Her unwavering determination to venture into the world, to admire the beauty of nature, and to embark on educational journeys is inspiring.

She is an ambitious and driven individual, always striving to create opportunities that benefit her entire family. The pursuit is rooted in her strong belief that every member of the family deserves to thrive and excel.

She is a natural leader with a strong desire to take charge and be involved in various activities. She has a confident and assertive personality. She is strong-willed in nature and has the ability to think independently and her inclination to express her thoughts and opinions. With a fiery determination, she always found the courage to speak her mind. With her unique perspective and the role, she played adds a dynamic dimension to our family dynamics. While her assertiveness may have sparked occasional conflicts, it has also fostered an environment of growth, understanding and the recognition that diverse perspectives enrich our collective experience.

5. Edgar — The Contented Spirit/ Dancing Dynamo (December 21, 1946)

His contented nature exudes a sense of peace and acceptance is remarkable. Free from the weight of ambition, he embraces life's simple pleasures and finds fulfillment in the present moment. His determination and belief in his abilities have led him to explore different avenues and find his own path in life, driven by a desire to create a better life for those he cares about. As an adventurous and free-spirited individual, he set out to explore the world and find new experiences.

Apart from his adventurous spirit, he is a talented dancer. His skills and passion for dancing and involvement in the University dance troupe gave him joy in expressing himself through movement.

He had the courage to embark on a journey that led him far from home. Starting a new business showcased his determination and entrepreneurial spirit.

He sees beyond the confines of conventional education and is willing to take risks in order to achieve his goals.

After three decades or more, he returned with his own family bringing a wealth of experiences. Over time, rekindled his connection with the family, particularly with our mother, showing a heartwarming reunion and appreciation for family ties.

6. Rebecca — The Heart of Harmony: Nurturer and Mediator.
(June 21, 1948)
(Author)

As a middle child, I straddled the line between older and younger siblings, offering guidance and support while seeking my own place in the family dynamics. This position allowed me to witness the joys, triumphs and struggles of both the older and younger generations, providing a unique perspective that shaped my understanding of our family as a whole.

Through my journey as a middle child in our family, I often found myself in the role of mediator and peacemaker. It was important to me to foster an atmosphere of harmony and understanding among my siblings. I came to embrace the beauty and significance of being the 6th child of 12. It afforded me the opportunity to bridge gaps, mediate conflicts and foster a sense of unity within our large family. I took the role of a caretaker, especially to our youngest sister. From her earliest days, I embraced the responsibility of watching over her, guiding her tender steps and providing a sense of security and love.

Being labeled as generous brought me great joy, not only in providing financial and material support but also in giving my time and effort to those I love. I have come to realize that true generosity lies not only in material possessions but in the profound connections we build with one another. I find immense joy in being able to contribute to the happiness and well-being of my family. For it is in these acts of kindness that I feel the truest fulfillment.

As I reflect on my journey, I find myself following in the footsteps of my mother, who raised 12 children single-handedly with unwavering determination and love. Similarly, I embarked on the path of single parenthood, raising my three children with the same values and principles my mother instilled in us; just like my siblings, my children have grown into accomplished professionals, each carving their own successful path in life.

Guided by the lessons of our mother, I have strived to impart the values of perseverance, compassion, and selflessness to my own children. The legacy of kindness and support that she instilled in us continues to be a guiding principle in our family.

While I may not claim to be a perfect author, I humbly acknowledge the profound impact my mother's legacy has had on shaping my role as a parent and the bond I share with my children. Through the trials and triumphs, I find solace in knowing that I continue the torch of resilience and love passed down by my remarkable mother.

7. Emiliano Jr. —Sports Maven / Legacy Keeper (October 13, 1949)

Blessed with striking looks and a proud soul, his generous spirit possesses a unique way of expressing his kindness and support to others. In those formative years, when financial limitations imposed constraints on dreams and aspirations, my brother carried the weight of unfulfilled possibilities. The lingering echoes of scarcity and a longing for financial stability shaped his perspective and fueled an inner drive to achieve success. It was within this intricate tapestry of emotions that the seeds of determination were sown.

His acts of generosity have touched the lives of many, extending beyond the boundaries of our family circle. His unwavering commitment to his friends is particularly noteworthy, as he goes above and beyond to offer support, both emotionally and materially. His act of generosity served as a declaration of triumph over adversity; through his accomplishments and generosity, Emiliano proved that triumphing over adversity can be a powerful force for good, and his actions became a symbol of hope and inspiration to all who knew him.

A sports enthusiast with a keen interest in tennis and boxing. He exhibits a deep passion for this sport, even traveling to prestigious events like the French Open and major boxing championships to witness them firsthand. He has a deep love for sports and is involved in organizing tournaments and sports teams and carried our father's sporting legacy. He shares our father's passion for sports and continues our father's tradition of promoting and supporting athletic endeavors. He established a tennis club named "EMGEN" Tennis Club, hosting tournaments on his personal tennis court that he graciously opened to the community. He is truly dedicated to following and enjoying these athletic pursuits, making them an integral part of his life and a source of inspiration.

He also has a talent for recollection of memories of the past anecdotes of our parents' love, discipline and passion for sports. He is someone who cherishes and preserves the family's memories, recollections and some old photographs from the past. His sentimental nature helps keep the family's stories alive.

8. Siegfredo — CheckMate: The Chess master/ Favorite Joker (March 13, 1951- September 23, 2015)

He was the perennial favorite among us and possessed a magnetic charm that lit up any room he entered. With a natural flair for humor and a mischievous twinkle in his eye, he was the embodiment of the family's jester. His love for numbers and his quick wit make him a source of endless entertainment, ensuring that laughter always resounds within our family's walls.

A multi-talented and accomplished brother with a passion for sports and gaming. He was a remarkable chess prodigy and an exceptional professional senior auditor of Aboitiz Shipping Corporation. With his keen strategic mind, he has clinched victory in chess tournaments every year during the company's sports festival; he reigns as a chess champion, alongside also a champion in table tennis and once in swimming contests. As a member of a private chess club, he was featured several times for winning in the tournaments sponsored by the club.

His intelligence and passion for chess shaped his life. His chess pursuit had impacted the richness of our family's experience. His dedication and skills led to his victories and recognition. His ability to think outside the box and pursue alternative avenues after he got sick demonstrated his resilience and determination to create a prosperous future for his family.

My brother's achievements brought joy and pride to our family and the inspiration he provided to other siblings. We celebrate his legacy as a role model and a cherished member of our family who will always be remembered with love and admiration.

9. Alexander — A Kaleidoscope of Life / The Charismatic Wordsmith, (January 4, 1952 - December 12, 2020).

In the tapestry of our family history, one stands out in vibrant color, depicting the life of my brother Alex. He was a man of contrasts —gifted with the acumen to excel academically and the charisma to captivate those around him. Gifted with a silver tongue, had the remarkable ability to sway hearts and minds with his eloquence. His charismatic presence and politician-like speech carry an air of magnetism that draws others in. Although his charm may occasionally lead him astray, his words possess a power that resonated within the hearts of those who heard them.

With intelligence that knew no bounds and a heart that sought to serve, his journey was a mosaic of triumphs and challenges. From excelling in academia to traversing distant lands in search of adventure, he left an indelible mark on the lives he touched. He had a natural charisma and a way of making people feel valued and appreciated, and his presence brightened the lives of many in the community.

Yet Alex's life was not without complexity. His reputation as a womanizer remains a bittersweet stroke in our collective memory. But it is in acknowledging this reality that we paint an honest portrayal of the man he was —complex, flawed, yet undeniably human.

From the classrooms where he shared knowledge to the far-flung corners where he sought adventure, he embraced life's palette with gusto. As we remember him, we celebrate his triumphs as an exceptional teacher, an accomplished embalmer/ manager, and a dynamic councilor, each brushstroke a testament to his brilliance. It was his unyielding spirit, his dedication to lifting others and his impact on the community that transcended the shapes of his life, leaving an enduring legacy.

10. Francz Gerrion: — A Piano Lover/ Chess Player /Silent Observer: (October 10, 1955)

With his quiet disposition, he observes the world with a discerning eye. He possesses a natural affinity for numbers and an entrepreneurial spirit that guides his ventures. While he may not be the loudest voice in the room, his perceptive nature and management-minded mindset contribute to his success in being financially independent. He is an enigmatic individual, preferring to keep his ventures close to his chest, yet his financial independence speaks volumes about his astute decisions and self-reliance.

An exceptional brother who has found his calling in the security industry, he takes charge of critical responsibilities, ranging from meticulously planning security operations to conducting thorough inspections. His unwavering dedication to ensuring the safety and protection of others is evident in the way he approaches his work with utmost professionalism and precision.

Apart from his professional achievements, he is not only a piano lover, but he also has a passion for sports. He finds joy and relaxation in playing basketball and engaging in strategic battles on the chessboard. These pastimes not only serve as a means of recreation but also sharpens his strategic thinking and decision-making skills, complementing his role in the security agency. Despite the demanding nature of his work and his involvement in sports, my brother remains approachable and caring. He never hesitates to lend a hand to those in need, making him not only a dedicated professional but also a compassionate human being.

11. Mona Liza -- The Modern-day Renaissance Woman/ Ultimate Globetrotter. (February 4, 1958)

Mona, the epitome of beauty and brains, embraces the ever-evolving world of modern technology with finesse. Her insatiable curiosity and innovative mindset lead her to explore new horizons and push the boundaries of what is possible. She effortlessly balances intelligence and elegance, inspiring those around her to embrace change and embrace their own potential.

Beyond her academic achievements, she possesses a keen eye for numbers and a natural talent for accounting and auditing. She possesses a meticulous and detail-oriented nature making her highly skilled in managing financial matters.

She is known for her accuracy, organizational skill and ability to provide insightful financial advice.

She is also an education advocate, supporting family members financially and ensuring that education remains a top priority in the family.

A wanderlust sister, ultimate globe trotter and avid photographer of nature's wonder. She has explored every nook and cranny of the United States, leaving footprints in every state, but her adventurous spirit doesn't stop there; she'd hopped from country to country, capturing the beauty of diverse cultures and landscapes through her lens.

Mona, our family's cherished historian and guardian of our heritage, assumes the significant responsibility of tracking our family tree with meticulous care and dedication. With unwavering commitment, she ensures that our roots are firmly anchored in our shared history and that our ancestors are preserved for generations to come. Her role extends beyond the mere recording of names and dates.

Beyond her dedication to documenting our family's history, her role as the introducer of new members cements her position as the bridge between generations.

Her meticulousness and attention to detail shine through as she meticulously updates our family's record, incorporating every birth, marriage, and milestone that shapes our shared journey. Through her tireless effort, our family remains connected across time and space, united by the threads of our shared ancestry.

As we reflect upon the immeasurable value of Mona's contribution, we are reminded of the importance of preserving our family's legacy. Through her diligent work, our family's story remains alive and vibrant, embracing both the past and the future with open arms.

12. Judith Leila — The Vibrant Life Saving Angel. / Endless Love Across Borders. (December 23, 1961)

In the chapter of our family's story, our youngest sibling is a shining light, illuminating the path of love, sacrifice and the resilience of the human spirit. Her selflessness has touched the lives of our entire family, reminding us of the extraordinary bonds that bind us and the power of unconditional love.

Through her selfless act, Judith not only gave our brother the gift of life but also reaffirmed the unbreakable ties that bind us as a family. As the youngest of our siblings, Judith radiates vibrant energy that fills every room she enters. With her natural talent for dance and choreography, she brings movement and rhythm to our lives. Her vivacious spirit serves as a constant reminder of the boundless possibilities that lie ahead, inspiring us to embrace life's twists and turns with unbridled enthusiasm. Beyond her remarkable act of organ donation, she continues to inspire us with her kindness, her unwavering support, and her ability to find beauty and meaning in even the smallest moments.

Her love knows no borders as she selflessly works abroad to ensure her family is well provided for, even if it means staying apart for an extended period. Judith acts as the pillar of support for her family, braving the challenges of working abroad to create a stable foundation for her loved ones.

She shows unwavering determination to provide for her family's needs. She is a guiding light and source of inspiration, reminding us that no distance can diminish the bond of a strong family foundation.

May we forever cherish the gift that Judith has given, and may her extraordinary act serve as a beacon of inspiration for generations to come. Her sensitivity, selflessness and her unwavering love continue to shape our lives, reminding us of the incredible power of familial bonds and the limitless potential of the heart.

Though I may not remember the exact moments of their births, I have come to cherish the unique qualities and the love that each of my siblings brought to our home. Together we formed a vibrant tapestry of personalities, dreams, and aspirations, all woven together by the unbreakable bond of family.

As I reflect on the diverse and unique personalities of each of my 12 siblings, I am stuck by the common thread that unites us all: our shared passions for dancing and sports. While we may have different interests, temperaments, and aspirations, there is something truly special about the way we all come together on the dance floor or the field.

No matter the challenges we face or the disagreements we have, the dance floor or sports arena has always been our refuge, a place where we can let go and express ourselves and find common ground. It is in these stages that our individual personalities fade into the background, and we become a united force, moving as one.

These shared passions have served as a source of joy, bonding and celebration throughout our lives, especially as we gather together in our much-anticipated family reunions or any getting-together events.

As I conclude this chapter, I am filled with gratitude for the 12 unique personalities that make up our family. I am in awe of my parent's resilience, patience and unwavering commitment. They fostered an environment where we learned to celebrate one another's successes, emphasize each other's struggles, and embrace the beauty of our differences. Their love transcended the boundaries of individuality, binding us together as a cohesive family unit.

CHAPTER 8
PASSIONS AND DEVOTIONS: THE JOYS AND FAITH OF OUR PARENTS

"Life without passion is not a life-it is merely an existence."

-Leslie Fieger

In this chapter, we delve into the various passions and interests that shaped our parents' lives and enriched their journey together. From the court to the chessboard, from the arena to the church pew, their pursuits reflected their individuality, bringing vibrancy and depth to their shared experiences.

Section 1: "The Spirit of the Game"

a. "The Basketball Enthusiast."

In the vibrant world of basketball, my father found his true passion; he was the best in his team. It was the cheers and the electric tournament that fate intervened and brought my parents together as my father showcased his skills, my mother, a cheerleader in the crowd, couldn't help but be captivated by his grace, determination and as he described in her diary, very handsome.

He took a role not only as a leader in the court but also organizing a team called "EMMO" EM for Emiliano, my father, and MO from my mother's name Monica.

He devoted countless hours to practicing, coaching and organizing basketball games and tournaments. Thru my father's leadership and skills, his ability motivated and inspired the players and instilled a sense of teamwork and sportsmanship, which led to the team's success. They won 2 championship trophies from the tournament in Dumanjug and Alegria, neighboring towns holding the basketball tournaments. These accomplishments made my father and our family proud, but most of all, the team members of his basketball who were so thankful for my father's dedication and commitment to the team.

b. Billiards and Strategic Mind

In the game of skill my father has another passion which is the game called Billiard. His adeptness in this game of skill in strategic thinking, precision shots, and the moments of friendly competition brought him both challenge and enjoyment in his life. In recollection, when we were very young, we used to fetch our father in the Billiard Hall when it was getting late at night per our mother's request.

c. Master of Chess

My father's fascination for the game of chess, his tactical prowess and the mental agility that he displayed on the chessboard illustrate his intellectual battles and the delight he found in unraveling the complexities of this timeless game. My brother Siegfredo inherited a passion for chess and was involved in chess tournaments.

d. "The Noble Art: Boxing, A Passionate Pursuit."

My father was an avid fan of boxing. He was kind of involved when our distant relative was one of the amateur boxers. He tries to be present during his training. My brothers Emiliano and Alex were the ones who my father took to boxing matches. My brother

Emiliano has a passion for boxing. As an avid fan of boxing, he never missed any Big Boxing fights till the present.

Section 2: A Taste of Adventure
"In the Arena of Cockfighting"

My father enjoyed exploring the world of cockfighting, a passion that immersed him in a realm of tradition, strategy and anticipation. Cockfighting plays a vital role in the life of Filipino men. It is called "Sabong" and is one of the Philippines' obsessions. He took some of my brothers to the arena where the sport is held. Mother was not in favor of this type of sport, but my father's excitement about the competition and camaraderie among fellow enthusiasts convinced her that his passion made him happy and gave her joy.

Section 3: In the Arena Of Politics: Family's Involvement

In addition to his other interests, my father has a passion for politics. My father's side of the family has the genes for political adventure. He was number #1 and the favorite councilor of our town. He was loved by the town folks, and he helped the community with the town's issues and concerns. He was compassionate, especially to the less fortunate in our town. He attends an official councilor session every Sunday.

My father's politics has influenced us as a united family in supporting his political endeavor. As a family, together, we help and anticipate every election helping in his campaign and our excitement going to election polls as we watch carefully during the manual counting of votes. It is always a celebration every time our father gets re-elected. My brother Alex, inspired by my father, followed a similar path in his own political tendencies. My father's political involvement has strengthened our bond as a family. We were all united in supporting my father's political passion.

Section 4: The Faith that Anchors; A Woman of Devotion"

My mother was raised Catholic, and her unwavering dedication to her Catholic faith was reflected in her deep spiritual connection, her commitment to prayers and attending mass, and the guiding principles that shaped her life; she made sure she devoted time to her faith enhancement through joining religious organizations for the community. She was a member of the Catholic Women's League and another religious group called "Sacred Heart of Jesus". Her devotion and her faith journey have instilled in us the values of Catholicism in our family; we all go to church on Sunday mass as a family. All of us siblings went to summer catechism and learned the teachings and traditions of the Catholic faith.

My mother's deep-rooted faith in Catholicism played a fundamental role in shaping her character and values. From a young age, she was instilled with a profound sense of devotion and reverence for God, which laid the foundation for her spiritual journey.

**Section 5: A Culinary and Creative Journey
"Passion for Cooking, Baking and Crochet"**

My mother loves to cook. Her noodles and chicken were so delicious. She excels in baking delicious sugar cookies and various cakes, constantly keeping herself engaged by experimenting with new recipes. In addition to nurturing her children and her busy teaching job, my mother found time for her passion which gave her satisfaction, and she passed it on to us with her recipes for torta, pansit and simple cakes. She claimed her love of cooking was after her mother's skill and experience in cooking. As far as her skill for crochet, it seems like none of us had the skill or interest.

Section 6: Melodies and Silver Screens
My Mother's Favorite Singer, Movies, and Dance Songs

Music and movies held a special place in my mother's heart. They were the threads that wove through the tapestry of her life, providing comfort, inspiration and a soundtrack to her cherished memories.

Movies like: Gone with the Wind, Queen of the Niles and Camelot held a special place in her heart, capturing her imagination and stirring her emotions with their compelling narrative and unforgettable performance.

But it wasn't just the movies that captivated her.; it was also the music that accompanied them. Certain songs became the soundtrack to her life, evoking a myriad of emotions and transporting her back to moments etched in her heart. One of the songs close to my parents' hearts is a song called "It's A Sin to Tell A Lie", a popular song in 1936 by Billy Mayhew. This song became more than just music; it became her cherished companion comforting her during challenging times and uplifting her spirits in moments of triumph. Another song she wrote in her diary is a popular Cebuano song, "Matud Nila", by Pilita Corales, a very popular Filipino singer. My mother loves all her songs.

My mother was also drawn to the rhythm of music from an early age. She expressed herself through dance which brought her joy and happiness. One of them is the "Dandansoy", a Filipino dance that she was passionate about. My mother always participates in dancing performances and in school events.

As I recollect my mother's favorite movies, singers, songs and dances, I am reminded of the deep connections they forged within our family.

These shared experiences not only enriched our lives but also provided a glimpse into the passions and interests that shaped my mother's character. Her favorite movies, singers and songs were a reflection of her vibrant personality, her appreciation for artistry, and her ability to find solace and inspiration in the world of entertainment.

In honor of my mother's favorites, I pay tribute to the joy and inspiration they brought into her life and the legacy they left behind.

Section 7: Family of Rhythm and Joy: Our Passion for Dancing and the Spotlight on the Dance Floor

As far as my recollection, adult members of the family never miss a town fiesta dance which everybody looks forward to every town festival year. I used to always dream that time would come when I am old enough to join my mother and my older sisters to the big town dance. It was a big honor to attend the dance, and our family always led the dances with my mother, who enjoyed every minute of it. We all enjoy the whole evening, and our family's presence on the dance floor always captures the attention and admiration of others. It was always one of my favorite memories and traditions. The town fiesta dance was a big deal that all the town folks were looking forward to. My uncles and cousins who come from other cities always attend with anticipation and excitement to this big celebration every year. Our house celebrates this fiesta with a houseful of guests with abundant food and drinks, and then everybody goes to the big dance event in the evening.

Our family loves to dance, and at every reunion and gathering, music and dancing are always part of our entertainment.

In these chapters, we witness the diverse interests and passions that colored our parent's lives. Their hobbies brought them joy, challenged their minds and created bonds with others who shared their enthusiasm. Equally significant was the steadfast faith that anchored them, shaping their values and inspiring a legacy of devotion that would resonate through generations to come.

CHAPTER 9

FIRM, FAIR AND LOVING: A MOTHER'S UNIQUE DISCIPLINE

"Discipline is the bridge between goals and accomplishments."

by Jim Rohan

In this chapter, we delve into the remarkable character of our mother, a woman whose firmness, intelligence, and unyielding determination left an indelible mark on our lives, from her tenacious approach to challenges to her unwavering dedication to her family. We celebrate the strength of her spirit and the impact she had on all of us.

Section 1: "Firmness in Action"

Within the tapestry of our family's memories, there exists an anecdote that illuminates the unwavering determination and firmness of our mother. It is a tale of a pivotal moment in my brother's life, Emiliano Jr., where his desire to fit in clashed with the reality of our family's financial circumstances. Through her firmness, our mother imparted a valuable lesson in resilience and instilled in my brother a strength that would guide him throughout his journey.

Anecdote: The Long Pants

When my brother turned 13, it was a town fiesta celebration; he wanted to attend the Town's Dance Night with anticipation and excitement, an event that held great significance for him and his friends. He was yearning for acceptance and the desire to be part of this social gathering.

When my brother mustered the courage to ask my mother for his pair of long pants to wear for the big night, my mother expressed financial constraints that prevented her from fulfilling my brother's request. My brother was so disappointed, and he tried to persuade my mother with his crying outburst. My mother stood firm in her decision despite my brother's plea.

My brother was frustrated and angry that he would miss out on the fun he would have with his friends. He spent his disappointment on the ground floor, stroking the roosters and crying.

Eventually, he developed a sense of understanding and the lessons he learned about perseverance, resilience, and the importance of making do with what one has.

This experience has had a lasting impact on my brother's character and his ability to navigate adversity throughout his life.

My mother's unwavering love and strength, through her firmness, provided my brother a powerful lesson and contributed to his personal growth.

This anecdote serves as a testament to the firmness and love of our mother, who, in the face of her son's disappointment, chose to impart a lesson of resilience. It illustrates the power of unwavering resolve and the lasting impact of her guidance. Through this experience, our mother equipped my brother with tools to navigate obstacles, teaching him the value of perseverance and the strength that comes from facing adversity with determination.

Ultimately, it is a testament to the unyielding love and wisdom of a mother who nurtures her children with both firmness and compassion.

Section 2: A Lesson In Humility. "A Mother's Feisty Request"

Within the tapestry of our family's memories, there exists an anecdote that encapsulates both the spirited nature of our mother and the lesson of humility it imparted on one of my brothers. It is a tale of a simple request that challenged his ego and pushed him outside of his comfort zone, revealing the unwavering love and strength of our mother's character.

Anecdote: The Market Run

One day, on a typical day at home where my brothers gather for lunch, my mother expressed her desire for my brother Emiliano to make a trip to the market and specifically request "ginamos," a dish that was considered less prestigious in the eyes of society, my brother's immediate reaction was "Why Me? His resistance and internal struggle with pride and him walking on the street with the dish in his hands. Just imagine my mother and brother's clash of wills. My mother reprimanded him for his open reluctance and gently tapped on his head, symbolizing a reminder of respect and obedience. With reluctance, he was forced to go to the market. During his journey, he experienced this internal battle between his pride and his deep-seated respect for our mother as he navigated the market.

My brother learned a lesson of humility and the strength of my mother's character. This seemingly trivial event had a lasting impact on his perspective, teaching him the importance of putting aside pride and embracing selflessness.

In reflection, my mother's request had a deeper meaning in her ability to challenge her children's perceptions and foster personal growth thru humbling experiences.

This anecdote serves as a reminder of the fierce yet nurturing spirit of our mother, who imparted valuable lessons with every interaction. It illustrates the power of a single moment, where pride was confronted, and a deeper understanding of humility was gained. Through her feistiness and unwavering love, our mother shaped not only our individual characters but also the collective fabric of our family's story. Ultimately, it is a tale of love, respect, and an enduring bond between a mother and her child.

Section 3: Feisty and Fearless: A Glimpse of Mother's Spirit

a. "A Woman of Purpose"

As I weave in the memories of actual anecdotes from our childhood, my sisters shared a story of the feisty side of my mother's character. This anecdote reveals her fiery resilience, the moments when she fearlessly stood up for what she believed in and protected her territory. This amusing and memorable anecdote showed her spirited nature. My father was a tall, handsome guy. It is not surprising that ladies could get attracted to him. When my feisty and determined mother learned about a woman trying to flirt and ride in our passenger truck from a certain location hoping to find father's presence, my smart and determined petite mother took off from work just to confirm her intuition and heard touches of rumors.

She went and took a ride in our truck unexpectedly and surprised the woman who routinely takes a ride in our passenger truck. She was hoping to find my father but had to face my mother.

My mother confronted the woman and introduced herself as the wife of the truck's owner, my father. Her undying love for my father was amazing. This incident illustrates her unwavering expectations and boundaries she sets and her dedication to her family, her passion for protecting what is rightfully hers is admirable. Her strength and determination to protect our family left a lasting impression on our family.

b. Determination and Grit

In her memoir, my mother recounts the countless moments her faith created a tapestry of love, support, and spiritual guidance.

As I reflect on my mother's journey, I am reminded of the powerful lessons she imparted through her unwavering commitment to her faith.

Through my mother's firm approach and determined spirit, she ensured that my father did not miss Sunday church before any cockfighting adventure, which was also held on the same days.

On some occasions, her feisty character shows when she threatens my father that the roosters do not take any precedence over our devotion and reaffirms the importance of faith and family in her life.

My father's love and respect for my mother were not mere obligations; they were the threads that wove his character, shaping him into a compassionate one. An empathetic husband he became.

As I reflect on my mother's journey, I am reminded of the powerful lessons imparted through her unwavering commitment to her faith.

Section 4: When Chores Await. "Mother's Expectation And Consequences"

Every day, before she went to school for her teaching job, her routine was leaving task lists for us to complete by the time she returned from work. The consequences of not fulfilling our responsibilities were receiving her signature pinch as a punishment.

Beyond the pinch itself, it was the underlying message that resonated with her children. We understood that her disciplinary actions were rooted in a genuine concern for our well-being and growth. The pinch became a symbol of accountability, a gentle reminder that our actions had consequences and that we were capable of making choices. It was through her unwavering commitment to instilling discipline that we grew to understand the value of self-control, responsibility, and the importance of adhering to rules.

In this chapter, we honor the formidable spirit of our mother, a force to be reckoned with. Her firmness, intelligence, determination, and occasional feistiness shaped our upbringing and prepared us for the challenges that lay ahead. Through the memories of actual anecdotes shared, we celebrate the impact of her character on our lives and the lasting lessons she imparted.

CHAPTER 10
OUR HOME: BEFORE MY FATHER'S STROKE, NURTURING DREAMS IN OUR HOMETOWN

"Home is the starting place of love, hope, and dreams." Home is where love resides, memories are created, friends always belong, and laughter never ends."

In the embrace of our home before the storm of life's challenges, we shared laughter, dreams, and unbreakable bonds that would carry us through the toughest of times.

In the pages to follow, I invite you to step back in time to a period of our lives that was filled with joy, laughter, and the warmth of family bonds. This chapter serves as a cherished tribute to the days when my father's smile and charm lit up every corner of our home and my mother's unwavering love and guidance shaped us into the individuals we would become.

Before my father's stroke, which forever altered the course of our lives, we were a close-knit family of 12, each sibling with our own unique personality and dreams. Our childhood days were filled with simple pleasures, and our home was a hub of lively activity. Amidst the laughter and occasional squabbles, one thing was constant: the love that bound us together.

Our parents put in relentless effort to support us and instilled within us the importance of diligence, reverence, and empathy. As I look back on those days, I am filled with gratitude for the love and care surrounding us, shaping the foundation of the life we would lead.

Join me now as we embark on a journey down memory lane. Revisiting the days before the stroke. As I share our family's stories, I hope to honor the legacy of my beloved parents and the spirit of togetherness that defined our lives. Let us celebrate the beauty of a time when our world was full of promise and hope, a time that will forever hold a special place in my heart.

Section 1. "Rhythms of the Past Memories From Our Home"

A. Harmonious Melodies: The Echoes. Of Piano Lessons.

In the realm of music, our family was a blend of formal education and natural talent. Our older sisters were the pioneers. They were fortunate enough to embark on a journey of formal piano lessons. Then, the piano lessons were extended to arranging a tutor at home to teach my two older sisters, Thelma and Jerry, the enchanting language of the piano right within the comfort of our home. My sister Thelma did not have an interest in learning as much as Jerry loved the lessons and grasped the passion for playing the piano.

This symphony of learning spilled over to our 3rd sister, Evangeline, who, under the tutorage of our mother, discovered the piano's secrets by ear, conjuring melodies that resonated with the very essence of her soul.

As the younger siblings, we became the captive audience to their musical performances. Our home echoed with their harmonious compositions, creating an indelible soundtrack to our upbringing. While I admire their prowess, I could not help but harbor a hint of envy. Amid the symphony that surrounded us, I forged for the chance to touch those ivory keys, to translate my emotions into music.

Some of the favorite titles of the music my sister Jerry plays through the piano were "Love and Devotion," "Remember Me,", "Daffodils", "Fur Elise," and many more.

On the other hand, my older sister Evangeline, who has the talent and skill of playing the piano by ear, has her favorite old songs." I'll be Seeing You, Till the End of Time, To Love Again, You Needed Me. Gaano Kita Kamahal, and all the songs that get us dancing, like Tango, Cha- Cha, and many more.

Their mastery became an inspiration, a reminder that music was not just a collection of notes but a language that transcended formal education. Each sister brought a unique tune to our family's ensemble, creating a rhythm of beauty and unity that remains etched in my memory.

B. Nocturnal Serenades: Nights Filled with Music And Romance

Amidst the quiet nights of our little town, a tradition would unfold that left a mark on my young heart. I was just a mere 9 or 10 years old, but those nights when a group of serenades would gather under the moonlit sky to sing their melodious tunes are etched vividly in my memory. Our house, bathed in the gentle glow of the moon, served as the stage for a serenade that was more than just music; it was a symphony of love, tradition, and community.

My beautiful young adult sisters peeked through our windows, captivated by the enchanting performance of the serenaders. The music flowed through the night, dancing on the gentle breeze, weaving its way into the souls of all who stood witness. The melodic tunes wrapped around our home, transforming it into a sanctuary of love and devotion.

As the final notes faded into the night, leaving behind an echo of love, our family stood united forever, touched by the enchantment of the serenade. It was a moment that captured the essence of our Filipino heritage, the beauty of tradition, and the power of music that ignited the flames of love.

Section 2: Balancing Love and Education

In the midst of our education-focused household, my mother exhibited a firmness that extended even into matters of the heart. As we navigated the challenges of adolescence, our relationship began to take shape, and with them, the curious dance of young love. My sisters, much like any teenagers, found themselves entangled in the allure of romance. However, my mother had a unique perspective on this chapter of our lives.

Amid the pages of our shared journey, a certain chapter stands out — a chapter filled with love letters, stolen glances, and the yearning of youthful hearts. For my sisters, this chapter was a delightful and at times tumultuous one, marked by the affectionate attention of young suitors. Yet, in the sanctuary of our home, my mother had woven an unwritten rule that governed these budding romances. No love letters allowed.

Her philosophy was clear: education was our foremost priority. Love, while important, was a distraction that she believed could wait. Thus, her "nonsense" approach extended to the matter of the heart. With a mixture of cunning and determination, my sisters devised creative ways to navigate her restrictions. Love letters were cleverly mailed to neighboring houses, escapades that would make for fond and amusing stories in years to come.

But behind the scenes, a deeper message resonated. My mother's stance on love was a testament to her dedication to our academic success. Her actions, though strict, stemmed from a place of unwavering love and a desire to secure our futures. As we navigated the labyrinth of relationships, we learned not only about love but about the value of priorities and the wisdom in balancing youthful passion with the responsibilities that awaited us.

My sisters may have had their secret rendezvous, but my mother's unyielding devotion to education was unwavering. It was a chapter of contrasts- a tale of stolen kisses and carefully orchestrated love letters that concealed themselves within the pages of our shared history.

Section 3: The Unforgettable Classroom: Our Mother's Firm but Fair Lessons/Recognitions

In the small town where we grew up, our elementary school had a special place in our hearts, not just because it was our first step into the world of education but also because it was where our mother, a dedicated teacher, imparted her wisdom to countless young minds, including her own children, in her classroom, there was no exception for familial ties -we were all treated equally, with her signature pinch serving as a gentle reminder that misbehavior would not be tolerated. Through her firm but fair approach, we learned essential life lessons that shaped us into the individuals we are today.

Our mother's classroom was a place of both learning and love. She welcomed all her students, including us, with open arms, fostering an environment where everyone felt valued and respected. Regardless of being her own children, we knew we had to adhere to the same rules and expectations as our classmates. There was no favoritism. We never expected any special treatment.

Her firmness in the classroom was balanced by her compassion and dedication to our education. She poured her heart into teaching, ensuring that each student, including her own, received the best education possible. Her passion for teaching ignited a love for learning within us and she instilled in us the value of hard work and perseverance.

In the realm of education, my mother stood as a beacon of excellence and dedication. Her passion for teaching was illuminated by her remarkable achievements, which were recognized far beyond the confines of our town. As a District Demonstrator, her expertise in English instruction, particularly reading, shone brightly. She instilled in her students a love for language and literature, nurturing their minds with the magic of storytelling and the power of words.

Beyond the classroom, her influence extended to the aesthetics of learning. Her commitment to nurturing the art of penmanship was evident in her students' handwritten work, a testament to the meticulous care she took in shaping young minds and hands.

But her impact was not confined to the classroom walls alone. With the same fervor she cultivated the fertile minds of her students, she cultivated lush and vibrant school gardens. Her hands, once guiding pens and pencils, now nurtured the soil, coaxing life from the earth and transforming the school grounds into living classrooms. Her dedication to environmental education, well ahead of her time, left us with lessons not only in botany but in stewardship and care for the world around us. She has the best garden in the whole elementary school.

Her recognition was more than just accolades; it was a testament to her unwavering commitment to her students' growth and her love for education. To us, her children, it was an affirmation of what we had known for a long time— that we were guided by a woman whose brilliance and heart lit up not only our home but countless young minds.

Her legacy as a teacher, demonstrator, and cultivator of knowledge continues to flourish in the hearts and minds of those she touched.

Section 4: A Memorable Summer in Baguio

In the midst of the bustling city life, my mother's journey took her to a different world— the enchanting hills of Baguio. It was the summer of 1963, a time when my older siblings were pursuing their education in Cebu City, and I was a 15-year-old high school student. Amidst the familiar routine of our lives, my mother embarked on an adventure that would etch itself into her heart forever.

Baguio Vocation Normal School became her sanctuary for fifty days, from April to May. A place where she honed her teaching skills and where she discovered a new side of herself. The cool breeze, the scent of the pine trees and the breathtaking scenery enveloped her every day. She often reminisced about those days with a sparkle in her eyes, sharing how she fell in love with the most beautiful city in the Philippines.

Yet, amidst her own growth and exploration, my mother didn't forget her responsibilities back home. Our youngest sister, a mere 16 months old, was entrusted to my care. As I juggled high school and my newfound role as a caretaker, a bond formed between us that would withstand the test of time. My mother's absence afforded me the chance to take on nurturing roles, transforming me into someone my younger sister could find solace in.

As the days went by, my father also joined her in Baguio, a testament to the unity and companionship that defined our family. Together, they embraced this chapter of their lives, mother in her pursuit of education, and my father in his unwavering support.

Looking back, that summer in Baguio was more than just an academic pursuit for my mother; it was a self-discovery, family unity, and a connection with nature's beauty.

The memories of those days have forever left an imprint on her heart, and the bond between me and the youngest sister, Judith, was forever solidified. The story of that summer is part of the tapestry that makes up the rich narrative of our family's journey.

This section serves as a reminder that amidst life's busyness, there are moments of serenity and growth that become cherished treasures, forever woven into the fabric of our lives.

Section 5: A Friendship Beyond Borders

In this section, I recount the story of Mara, a Peace Corps volunteer who had an integral part of my mother's life during the exchange program. Mara was assigned to the elementary school where my mother was teaching. Her class was picked as part of the program. They both share passion for teaching and their dedication to making a difference in the lives of students.

Mara's presence and assistance impacted my mother's teaching methods and the student's learning experience. They became friends and spent time together both inside and outside the classroom, showcasing the camaraderie and exchange of knowledge between the two.

Mara used to refer to my mother's family as "Cheaper By The Dozen" My mother embraced the reference with pride, seeing it as a testament to her dedication to education and nurturing the young minds.

My mother learned from Mara's global perspective and their friendship was enriched with her own understanding of different cultures and teaching methods. At the same time Mara's experience broadened her knowledge of Filipino culture, especially their unwavering hospitality. During her time with my mother, she learned the art of gardening with my mother's assistance.

Their friendship continued even after Mara's departure and my mother's teaching approach was influenced by the insights and experiences they shared.

Section 6: The Sacred Tradition of "BLESS"

In our family, a tradition that has stood the test of time flows through our veins — the tradition of "BLESS" This simple yet profound gesture embodies our respect for our elders, a practice that has transcended generations and etched itself into the fabric of our family's identity.

From the very moment one crosses the threshold of our home, "BLESS" becomes an unspoken but deeply ingrained protocol. Regardless of age or relation, each member approaches the elders and gently touches their hand to their forehead. It is a gesture that requires no words, a silent acknowledgement of the wisdom, experience, respect and love that our elders bring to our lives.

"BLESS" isn't just a word; it's a bond that unites us. It's the bridge that connects the young with the old, the new with the seasoned. It's a thread that ties us back to our ancestors reminding us the values they upheld and the legacy they left behind. Through "BLESS," we honor our grandparents, aunties, and uncles, acknowledging their role as pillars of guidance and wisdom.

In our home, my mother's voice would ring out, reminding us of the significance of "BLESS". She would remind us that this simple act was a way of nourishing the bonds that held our family together. It was a ritual of love, respect, and unity, a small but profound gesture that encapsulated our devotion to one another.

As we continue to uphold the tradition" BLESS "we carry forward the essence of our ancestors, their teachings, and their values. It is a reminder that even in a rapidly changing world, some things remain constant — the importance of family, the value of respect, and the power of connection. Through "BLESS" we touch the past, honor the present, and forge a path toward the future, bound by the threads of love and tradition.

In a world where traditions often fade away, "BLESS" remains a steadfast beacon in our lives. It's a cherished reminder that the simplest gestures can hold the deepest meaning, and that by honoring our elders, we honor the very essence of who we are as a family.

Section 7: Guiding Lights of Faith: Family Prayer, Church, and Catechism

In the heart of our bustling family life, one constant thread connected us all— our faith. From the early days of childhood to the bustling teenage years, the cornerstone of our upbringing was the strong foundation of faith. It wasn't just about attending Sunday mass or memorizing prayers; it was a tapestry woven with moments of family prayer, church rituals and the summer embrace of catechism classes.

a. Family Prayer- The Heartbeat of our Home

Gathered around the table or in a room, our parents would lead us in prayers that whispered hope, strength, and gratitude. These sacred moments taught us the importance of seeking guidance, giving thanks and strengthening the bonds that held us close.

b. Sundays at the Church- A Day of Reverence

Every Sunday was a pilgrimage of sorts-a journey to the church that stood as a testament to our shared faith. The pews we occupied were not just benches; they were sanctuaries where we learned to listen, reflect and draw inspiration.

c. Catechism - Lessons Beyond the Classroom

When summer arrived, it wasn't just about break from school. It was the season of growth for our faith formation. Catechism classes were our windows to understanding the intricacies of our faith, guided by dedicated teachers who imparted not just knowledge but a genuine love for God's teachings. The warmth of those classrooms and the friendships formed there remain etched in our hearts. The classes are held in the morning and every afternoon we attend the mass for Flores de Mayo.

Our faith journey was a tapestry of family prayer, church gathering, and summer catechism classes. It was more than just a set of rituals; it was a compass that guided us through life's challenges and joys. As we move forward, those early lessons continue to illuminate our path, a legacy of faith that we treasure and pass on to the next generation.

Section 8: A Home Filled with Generations of Love

In the heart of our bustling household, amidst the laughter of my 12 siblings and the myriad of activities that defined our home, stood the unwavering presence of our beloved grandmother. She was more than just a matriarch; she was a guiding light, a source of comfort, and a repository of wisdom that shaped our family's destiny.

My mother's dedication to family was remarkable, but it reached new heights when she welcomed our dear grandmother into our home. With the passing of our grandfather, my mother took on the responsibility of caring for her even as she continued to raise her own children. The bustling atmosphere of our household did not deter my mother; instead, it infused our home with a deep sense of togetherness.

As a child, I vividly remember the warmth of my grandmother's presence. She had a quiet kindness that radiated, enveloping us all in an embrace of unconditional love. Her gentle hands created masterful dishes that would become family favorites and her stories wove a tapestry of our heritage, connecting us to generations that came before.

I was fortunate to spend my early high school days under her roof, learning not only the secrets of her kitchen but also the values she held dear. Those days in her house were an immersion in tradition and love, an experience that left an indelible mark on my heart.

Through my mother's devotion and our grandmother's presence, our home became a sanctuary where different generations mingled, shared stories, and drew strength from one another. The lessons of compassion, selflessness and respect that my mother demonstrated echoed the legacy of our grandmother, forming the foundation which our family thrived.

Through the lens of time. It's clear that my mother's commitment to caring for our grandmother was a testament to her unyielding love, a love that extended beyond her own children to embrace the generations that came before and those that would follow.

And so in the pages of this memoir, I honor my mother's dedication and the warmth of our grandmother's presence. Their bond and their influence remind me that family is not simply about shared blood; it's about shared stories, shared values, and shared love that spans across generations, leaving an enduring legacy of love and unity.

Section 9: A Home of Helpers and Harmony: Before My Father's Stroke

In the tranquil days before the stroke, our home was a haven of both bustling activity and serene calm. A testament to our family's hard work and dedication, we were fortunate enough to have a few hired helpers who contributed to the rhythm of our daily lives. Their presence was more than just a convenience; it was a reflection of the unity and shared responsibilities that defined our household.

These helpers became part of our extended family, their laughter and camaraderie interwoven with the fabric of our everyday routines. From assisting in the kitchen to tending to household chores, they were unseen hands that supported our parents in managing the bustling household of 12 siblings. Their role was crucial in maintaining the harmony that echoed within our walls.

The support of these helpers not only eased the physical burden on our parents but also served as a reminder of the values we held dear—empathy, cooperation and gratitude. The pre-stroke era was characterized by a sense of abundance, where the presence of helpers enhanced our quality of life and allowed us to focus on the joys of childhood and growth. The legacy of our home of helpers and harmony lives on as a cherished foundation upon which we continue to build our lives.

Section 10: A Joyous Union and the Gift of Grandparenthood

As life continued to unfold, new chapter emerged within the tapestry of our family's journey, it was marked by my sister's marriage, a milestone that brought both joy and reflection to our household. She was the first among us to find a partner, a choice that resonated with youth and vitality.

While some might have deemed my sister's choice to marry at a young age unconventional, my parents' heart held an understanding that transcended conventional norms. Their support was not only rooted in love but also in the recognition that life's journey is a patchwork of diverse experiences, each contributing to the vibrant tapestry of our existence.

With the union came the prospect of a new generation. It wasn't long before the rhythm of life welcomed the pitter-patter of tiny feet, announcing the arrival of our family's first grandchild. The birth of Jessica was a momentous occasion that embraced my parents in a sea of indescribable happiness.

As I reflect upon these events, I am reminded that our family's journey is a mosaic of moments, each etching itself into the core of our being. Yet bonds of matrimony and arrival of a grandchild brought our family together in celebration and unity.

However, as life's journey took an unforeseen turn with the stroke, the dynamics of our household would undergo a profound transformation. The changes that followed would test our resilience, illuminate the strength of our bonds, and propel us forward into a new chapter- one that was defined by challenges, but also the unwavering spirit that had always been a hallmark of our family.

CHAPTER 11
GUIDING WISDOM: LESSONS FROM MAMA

"Her wisdom illuminated our path, showing us the way even in the darkest moments"

In this chapter, we delve into the wisdom that our beloved mother left behind us. Through her diaries, we find her heartfelt reflections on life, values, and the principles she hoped to instill in her children. These timeless lessons serve as a testament for her enduring love and enduring influence on our lives.

Section 1: Trust and Integrity

"Can be trusted in words and deeds"

In her words, Mama emphasized the importance of trustworthiness. She knew that one's words and actions define character, and she hoped we would uphold honesty and integrity in everything we do. Through her example, she showed us the power of reliability and the value of a steadfast heart.

Section 2: Financial Responsibility

"Not to spend more than what you earn"

Mama's frugality and financial wisdom were cornerstones of her life. She believed in living within one's means and managing resources responsibly. Her advice to avoid overspending and to embrace practicality was a lesson in self -sufficiency and foresight. Her teachings remind us that true wealth lies in financial prudence and a contented heart.

Section 3: Helping others

"Lend a helping hand to those who are in dire need"

Generosity was at the core of Mama's teachings. Her compassionate heart taught us to extend a helping hand to those less fortunate. Her message was clear; kindness knows no boundaries, and even the smallest act of goodwill can make a significant impact. Mama's legacy of kindness continues to guide us in making a positive difference in the lives of others.

Section 4: The Rewards of Diligence

"Lazy people want much but get little, but those who work hard will prosper and be satisfied."

Through her own experiences, Mama understood the value of hard work and determination. She recognized that success comes to those who put in effort and persevere. With this wisdom, she encouraged us to chase our dreams, with diligence and tenacity, knowing that the rewards of honest labor bring not just prosperity but also a sense of fulfillment.

Conclusion

As we reflect on those lessons Mama left for us, we are reminded of the enduring impact she has on our lives. Her teachings, written with love in her diaries. continue to guide us through challenges and triumphs. Through her words, Mama remains a guiding light, inspiring us to live lives of trust, prudence, compassion, and diligence-just as she had hoped.

CHAPTER 12
FROM HOME TO CITY: EDUCATION, SACRIFICE, AND GROWING UP

"Education is the key that unlocks the golden door of freedom and opportunity" - George Washington Carver"

As the vibrant city lights of Cebu beckoned, our family embarked on a new chapter filled with hope, dreams and sacrifices. The time had come for my siblings to pursue their college education, venturing beyond the familiar comforts of our hometown. It was a bittersweet moment as we bid farewell to the embrace of our loving parents, who wholeheartedly believed in the power of education. This unwavering dedication and selflessness set the stage of this transformative journey that shaped our lives.

In this chapter, I invite you to join me on a reflective exploration of adolescence, marked by the pursuit of knowledge and the sacrifices we made along the way. From the bustling city streets to the hallowed halls of academia, we discovered the boundless opportunities that awaited us.

Through heartfelt anecdotes, cherished memories, and glimpses into the dynamics of our family, we will delve into the sacrifices made by our parents to ensure that each of us could grasp the transformative power of education. We will witness the triumphs and tribulations, the moments of joy and moments of longing, as we strived to create a better future for ourselves and honor the dreams our parents held so dear.

Section 1: Before My Father's Stroke

In the early years of our education journey, our parents worked tirelessly to provide us with opportunities for learning and growth. Their unwavering support and sacrifices paved the way for the first five siblings to pursue their careers and dreams. Each step of the way was filled with hard work, determination and the knowledge that education held the key to a better future.

In the pursuit of education, our family's journey took a significant turn when it came to my older siblings. They were determined to continue their studies in the city, which meant a whole new world of challenges and opportunities. Leaving behind the comforts of our rural home, they embark on a new chapter of their lives.

Finding suitable accommodation in the city was no easy feat for my parents who worked tirelessly to secure a place for my siblings. A two-bedroom house became their sanctuary, a place where dreams and aspirations were nurtured amidst the bustling urban life. Our parents, knowing the importance of sustenance during their academic pursuit, made sure that they never went hungry. Every week, packages filled with provisions like rice, bananas, and sweet potatoes were sent through the bus and dropped at the doorsteps.

In the little house they were not alone. A helper was there to provide support, ensuring that they had essentials for their studies. This newfound independence came with its own set of challenges and triumphs, as they navigated city life while upholding the values instilled in them by our parents.

Through their dedication and hard work, my older siblings emerged as beacons of inspiration for our family. Their educational journey wasn't just about textbooks and lectures; it was a testament to the sacrifices made by our parents, the determination of my siblings, and the unbreakable bond that held us all together.

A. Thelma's Education Journey

In the journey of education that unfolded within our family, my oldest sister, Thelma, stood out as the trailblazer. With a stroke of fortune, she had the privilege of attending a private school, St. Theresa's School, where she took her Secretarial course. She also plays piano through formal lessons. She was the first among us to tread an educational path. She was 19 years old and got a job in the City Hall in the Department of Water district. While working she went to night school to pursue a bachelor's degree and graduated with a Bachelor of Science in Elementary Education from the University of the Visayas in 1964. She tried teaching for a while and found out it was not really her calling and instead stayed in her job for 28 years till she retired.

B. Leo's Educational Path

Our oldest brother, the second sibling, Leo graduated from the University of San Carlos with a degree in Junior Geodetic Engineer. My brother passed the Board of Geodetic Engineering with flying colors in 1964. He was the quiet type and intelligent with no problems in school or any issues related to his pursuit to college education. He had some dry humor sometimes but was always an observer. He got employed after his graduation in a government court office. He kept the job until he retired.

The Legacy of Education: A Parent's Guidance in Choosing a Path

As I delve deeper, into the pages of my mother's memoir, it becomes evident that our family's journey has not been without its own share of challenges and complexities. Among the many chapters that form the tapestry of our lives, there lies a story of unfulfilled dreams and lingering resentment.

As they meticulously weighed the financial realities and long term prospects, their ultimate goal remained steadfast: to ensure that each of their children had the opportunity to pursue education without compromise.

For my sisters however, the chosen path felt like a restriction on her dreams and ambition. The resentment took root, fueled by a longing for a different course that seemed tantalizing out of reach. While our parents' decisions were guided by love and the desire to provide for the family's collective future, it was undeniable that individual aspirations sometimes took a backseat.

When it came to my older sisters' future paths their decisions to pursue teaching careers were not entirely of their own volition. Instead, they were influenced by a delicate interplay of circumstances and familial expectations.

Reflecting on our family's educational journey, I am aware of the mixed emotions and challenges that arose when it came to deciding our career paths. While my parents had the best intentions in guiding us towards education, it wasn't always a smooth process, particularly for my two older sisters, the 3rd and 4th siblings, Jerry and Evangeline, the choices made for their careers sparked feelings of resentment that still lingered.

My older sisters with their boundless aspirations held a deep longing to pursue a career in nursing. However, amidst the choices and decisions that shaped our lives, my mother, guided by her own experiences and circumstances, encouraged my sisters to pursue a different path - that of teaching, a profession highly valued by my parents and they want Jerry and Evangeline to carry on.

C. Jerry's Path to Knowledge

As for my sister, Jerry, despite her disappointment and resentment she accepted our parents' decision and turned it into a positive journey. She became a good teacher and loved her profession at the end. She graduated from Cebu Normal School, our mother's choice which was her Alma Mater. My sister got her degree in Bachelor of Science in Elementary Education. Immediately after her graduation, she got her first teaching job in one of the remote barrios in Moalboal in 1964.

D. Evangeline's Academic Achievements

The weight of unfulfilled dreams cast a shadow upon my sister's heart, and with each passing year, the embers of resentment smoldered within her. Despite her highest achievements and the success, she attained in her teaching career, there remained a lingering sense of what could have been.

In exploring my sister's educational journey, we are reminded of the intricate web of love, sacrifice, and personal growth that binds a family together.

My sister's experience in education gave her valuable skills that she might not have gained in other careers.

Her determination turned a career that wasn't her first choice into a successful and fulfilling journey. She graduated in Cebu Normal School and got the Bachelor of Science of Elementary Education. Then she got her Master's degree. Through her dedication and perseverance, she made an impact on helping her students and her teachers later as a Public School Supervisor. She achieved the highest academic education, Doctor of Education Ed.D.

My sisters eventually embraced their roles as educators and found fulfillment in their professions.

E. Edgar: Educational Journey of Independence

The second brother of the family studied his college education in the University of the Visayas. He started teaching education but in his 3rd year college, he had a change of heart. He decided to leave his college education behind and venture into a new city for his own pursuits. He embraced the challenges of starting his own business and building a life independently. Away from home for years, my mother's heart couldn't help but ache. In her eyes, I saw the weight of a mother's concern. Yet, even in her worry, my mother managed to find a quiet strength. She has raised us to be independent, to embrace life's uncertainties, and so she had to extend the same lessons to herself. She reminded herself that her son was carving his own path, just as she had taught him to.

In conclusion, as I look back on those years before the stroke, I am filled with a deep sense of gratitude for the sacrifices and determination that defined our family's journey. We navigated through challenges, supported each other's dreams, and held unto the values our parents instilled in us.

Little did we know that the stroke would mark a turning point in our lives, altering the path we were on. Yet amidst the uncertainties that followed, the foundation of education and unwavering unity we had built served as a guiding light. Each sibling's journey, unique as it was, was rooted in the lessons of love, perseverance and the value of education that were sown during those precious years.

Looking back, I am reminded that our shared aspirations, boundless support, and my mother's unwavering dedication laid the groundwork for the accomplishment and milestone that were to come.

As we faced the challenges of the future, the lessons learned during our time before the stroke remained a beacon of strength , reminding us that together, we could weather any storm and be stronger as one.

CHAPTER 13
THE JOURNEY THROUGH ADVERSITY: A NEW CHAPTER BEGINS

"Life is not about waiting for the storm to pass, but about learning to dance in the rain."-by Vivian Greene

In the midst of life's unanticipated turns, our family was faced with a significant challenge that would test our resilience and unity. The stroke that befell our 52-year-old father marked a pivotal moment in our lives, causing ripples of change that extended to every corner of our family tapestry. As we delve into this chapter, we'll not only explore the physical and emotional aspects of this event but also understand how it influenced the trajectory of our educational pursuits, shaping our mother's decisions and sacrifices.

A Memoir of my Mother's Voice

"In 1964, my beloved suffered his first stroke. I can still remember the worry that settled over our home like a heavy fog, clouding our days with uncertainty. He spent an entire month in the hospital, battling against the odds to regain strength. Each day felt like a silent prayer, a plea to God for his recovery,

When the news finally came that he was out of danger, relief washed over us like a gentle wave. I thanked God with every fiber of my being for giving us this precious second chance. But as the days turned into weeks and weeks into months, I realized that the ordeal had left its mark not only on my husband's health but on our family's stability as well.

I found myself grappling with a nervousness that I had never experienced before. The weight of medical bills, the uncertainty of his future health, and the responsibility of raising our 12 children seemed to press down on my shoulders. I knew that I had to be strong for him, for our children, and for myself. But the reality of our situation was a constant reminder of the fragility of our financial standing.

It was during this time that I truly began to understand the power of resilience and determination. I had always believed that challenges were meant to be overcome, but this was a lesson that tested the depths of my convictions. I was determined not to let this setback define us or dictate our path forward.

As I stood at the crossroads of uncertainty and hope, I knew that I had to find a way to stabilize our family's financial institution. I embarked on a journey that would lead me to make some of the toughest decisions in my life. With my 12 children by my side, each of them a testament to the love and life my husband and I had built, I set my sights on a future that would honor his legacy and secure our family's well-being.

Looking back now, I see how that challenging period molded us into the strong, united family we are today. The lessons of those days continue to guide me, reminding me that in the face of adversity, love and determination can light our way. And so I write these words not only to remember the struggles we faced but to honor the resilience that carried us through."

Section 1: A Sudden Twist of Fate

At the heart of our family's story lies a turning point that forever altered the course of our lives. It was a moment that brought us face to face with the fragility of existence and the indomitable strength of the human spirit. The stroke that struck our father was more than a medical event; it became a catalyst for a journey of resilience, love, and transformation that would define the years to come.

Section 2: The Road to Recovery

As the weeks passed, a new journey commenced, one marked by recovery, determination, and unwavering perseverance. Our father's commitment to his physical therapy served as a powerful testament to his willpower, guiding him through every challenge, with each step marking a victory over adversity. Our 46-year-old mother, the unflinching cornerstone of our family, stood beside him, providing steadfast support and boundless love.

Section 3: A Changed Dynamic

With time, we witnessed the evolution of our family's dynamics. Our father emerged from the shadow of his stroke, reshaped but not broken. His speech, though altered, carried a newfound depth, a testament to his spirit's unwavering strength. Our daily lives found a new rhythm, one marked by small victories and cherished moments that took on renewed significance.

When unexpected challenges emerged on our family's path, our lives took an unforeseen turn. The untimely stroke that befell our beloved father shook the foundation of our household, leaving us grappling with uncertainty. As we navigated through this difficult time, we discovered a newfound resilience within us. With our mother at the helm, we embraced change, adapting our dreams and aspirations to the shifting tides. Education became not just an individual pursuit but a collective endeavor, binding us together in the face of adversity.

In the face of this challenge, our family's unity became our greatest asset. Each member stepped forward, shouldering responsibilities and offering support in their unique ways. Our father, determined to contribute, found innovative avenues to support our mother, his indomitable spirit inspiring us all.

Section 4: Continuing the Journey: A Legacy of Strength

As the months turned into years, our father's journey through recovery forged a legacy that would guide us through life's trials. His resilience, unbreakable love, and tenacity to forge ahead left an indelible mark on us. His journey taught us that adversity can be transformed into opportunity, that strength can be discovered in vulnerability, and that love remains the unshakable foundation upon which our family thrives.

In the face of challenges, our family emerged stronger and more bonded than ever before. Our father's stroke was not just a chapter of difficulty. It demonstrated how the human spirit could triumph over adversity, leaving behind a lasting legacy of strength, resilience, and love.

CHAPTER 14
NAVIGATING CHALLENGES AND TOUGH CHOICES: SIBLING RESENTMENT AND MOTHER'S SACRIFICES

"Adversity has the remarkable ability to reveal both our strengths and vulnerabilities. In the face of tough choices, resentment may arise, but beneath it lies the unwavering love that binds families together."

In life, decisions are made based on circumstances and necessities, often with the best intentions at heart. As we journey through the tapestry of our family's history, retain chapters stand out where emotions ran high, and choices were made that left an indelible mark on us all. This chapter delves into the complex web of feelings and decisions that shaped our family dynamics during financial strain and sacrifice.

Our family's story is a tapestry woven with love, sacrifice, and the complexities of human emotions. In these pages, we explore a chapter that delves into the heart of our family dynamics, a period where our mother's difficult decisions, made out of love and necessity, left some of us wrestling with emotions that lingered for years.

Section 1. Education in Flux

At the time of our father's stroke, each of us siblings were at different stages of our educational journey. At this time, our oldest siblings, Thelma (24), Leo (23), and Jerry (22) were already earning. Evangeline (19) had just graduated from college, Eddie (18) just started college, and Rebecca (16), I had just graduated from high school and was ready to attend a pre-nursing course, a career chosen by my mother. The rest of my younger siblings, Emiliano Jr. (15), Fred (13), and Alex (12) were still in high school, and Francz (9), and Mona Liza (6), all still in the elementary grades, and Judith was still a toddler.

The future we had envisioned was suddenly clouded with uncertainty, and its financial implications became apparent.

Section 2: Resentment Unveiled

As each of us pursued our own educational path, my mother's sacrifices manifested in various forms. As the specter of financial instability loomed after our father's stroke, our mother found herself at a crossroads, making choices that would influence not only our education but also cause a rift among us. From my mother's decision to redirect my sisters' paycheck to cover our college tuition (especially for my tuition, who was the only one ready to go to college) to finding ways to make ends meet, she demonstrated an unwavering commitment to our future. However, my siblings didn't always fully understand these sacrifices, leading to lingering resentment that continues to echo in our family dynamics. These feelings were born from a sense of inequality, misunderstood intentions, and the weight of our own struggles.

Section 3: Understanding the Anguish

To truly comprehend the depth of these feelings, we must strive to understand the emotions that fueled them. Imagine the frustration of feeling that my sisters' needs were overlooked and that their own paths were obscured by financial concerns. Even though these emotions are complicated, they are genuine and should be recognized. To truly grasp the depth of these emotions, it's essential to step into the shoes of those who harbored resentment. The reasons behind their feelings are complex, rooted in a sense of perceived inequality and misinterpreted intentions. This period became a chapter of strife and struggle, with emotions running high as education clashed with the delicate dance of financial stability.

In this chapter, I 'll also address my attempts to bridge the gap between my mother's intentions and my siblings' feelings. As a narrator, I 'll express my gratitude for the opportunities my education afforded and my understanding of their frustrations. My goal is to emphasize that while the choices my mother made may have caused tension, they were made with the utmost care for our future.

Section 4: Reflections on Sacrifices

As we unravel the threads of our mother's sacrifices, let us remember that her actions were born from a place of her devotion. She navigated uncharted waters, trying to ensure our collective future even in the face of financial strain. The decisions she made were never meant to create division but rather to build a foundation on which we could all stand.

Section 5: Transformation through Understanding

The years have gifted us with hindsight, and with it comes the ability to understand the circumstances that molded those decisions. The resentment that once felt all-consuming begins to transform into a poignant reminder of the complexity of family life. It is a testament to the depth of our emotions and our journey through both triumphs and tribulations.

Section 6: Unity and Moving Forward

Now, as we reflect on those days and the ensuing years, we find strength in the unity that prevails. Each sibling's contribution, whether financially or emotionally. In acknowledging these emotions, we can create a space for healing and unity. Our mother's legacy is not only one of sacrifice but of love that transcends even the most challenging moments.

Our family's history is not defined solely by the choices made in times of challenge but by our collective ability to heal, understand, and come together. While the scars of resentment may linger, they are overshadowed by the love that ultimately unites us, transforming once-bitter memories into lessons that strengthen our family's enduring tapestry.

Section 7: Shared Strength: Sibling Support in the City

In the wake of my father's stroke, our family faced a new reality, one that required us to make adjustments and sacrifices we hadn't anticipated. As my younger sibling pursued a college education in the city, the financial burden fell heavily upon my mother's shoulders. Determined to see us through, she found a way to make ends meet, even if it meant relying on our extended family support.

In addition to my sisters' help, who were already working in their teaching profession in Moalboal, Jerry and Evangeline's paycheck was redirected to our college tuition; my sister Thelma, resourceful and resilient, rented a small room in the city where our uncle and his family resided. It was a tight squeeze, but we made it work. She and I share that room while my brothers set up their makeshift sleeping quarters in the basement. Our lives had changed drastically, but we embraced the situation with a sense of unity and shared purpose.

With a dedication fueled by necessity, my brother and I walked to the university each day during my pre-nursing years. We were determined to lighten the financial load on our mother's shoulders. I found opportunities to contribute, offering babysitting services to my cousin's daughter and providing tutoring to our neighbor's son. Every bit helped, and in doing so, we were not only easing the financial burden but also reaffirming our commitment to our family.

As we embarked on this new chapter of our lives after my father's stroke, we encountered challenges that tested our resilience and resourcefulness. Rainy days often brought an unwelcome guest to our basement—flooding. Our brothers, who had set up their sleeping quarters there, had to contend with rising waters and the discomfort that came with it. It was a reminder that adversity could come in unexpected forms, but we faced it head-on, finding ways to mitigate the impact and remain undeterred.

Our makeshift kitchen in the basement, once a place of warmth and nourishment, required creative improvisation. The flooding meant we had to adapt our cooking routine, preserving our meals and the little comforts we held dear. It was a vivid illustration of how even the simplest tasks became feats of ingenuity in the face of adversity.

In those trying times, my older sister emerged as a pillar of strength. Thelma, being the only one working in the city, took on the responsibility of not only funding our shared living space but also hiring a helper to alleviate the burdens of daily tasks. Her dedication was a testament to her commitment to our family's well-being, and her wages helped ensure that we had the assistance we needed to manage our home during those challenging days.

As the days turned into weeks and the weeks into months, we navigated the new path with determination. We were no strangers to challenges, having been raised in an environment that celebrated hard work and unity. Our collective sacrifices were a testament to our family's strength and resilience, as well as a reflection of the unwavering love that bound us together.

Through the shared struggles, our bond grew stronger. We relied on each other's strength and found solace in the unwavering support we provided. It was a period that illuminated the depth of our unity and our ability to confront hardship with resilience.

Section 8: Navigating Dreams and Finances: My Nursing Internship

As the days counted down to the start of my nursing internship, a mixture of excitement and anxiety coursed through my veins. It was a dream come true, a significant milestone on my journey to becoming a registered nurse. My acceptance into the internship program was a cause for celebration, but it also brought forth a fresh wave of financial concerns. It was a pivotal time for my family, especially after my father's stroke, which had already shifted the financial landscape.

In the midst of my anticipation for the internship, I knew that my mother was just as elated as she was apprehensive. The prospect of my growth and success was met with the reality of the expenses involved. With a heavy heart, I could sense the weight of her worries- the tuition fees, the expenses that accompanied my studies, and the ongoing medical costs for my father's care.

Throughout the years, my mother's determination had propelled us forward, surmounting challenges with resilience and grace; as I prepared to step into the world of nursing, I was not only taking my first steps towards a fulfilling career but also navigating the financial complexities that came with it. The road ahead was uncertain, yet my mother's unwavering support was a constant reminder that I was not alone.

As I left for the nursing dormitory, I carried not only my excitement and dedication but also the weight of my family's hopes and dreams. This chapter unveils the intricate dance between ambition and financial constraints, shedding light on the sacrifices my mother made and the determination that united us in facing uncharted waters.

In those challenging times, as I embarked on my nursing internship, the weight of my education expenses rested on a delicate balance. My mother's worry was palpable, and in the midst of it all, there was an unspoken truth that my sisters' paycheck would, in part, contribute to my tuition and support. It was a reality that brought with it a mixture of emotions. For my sister, it was a sacrifice that wasn't met without its own share of resentment, an undercurrent of silent struggles. I understood her feelings even though they remained unspoken. Yet, intertwined with the tension, was a stronger thread of love and unity, a testament to the bonds that held our family together even in the face of financial strain.

CHAPTER 15
NAVIGATING LOSS AND RENEWED STRENGTH: REMEMBERING OUR FATHER

"Though nothing can bring back the hour of splendor in the grass of glory in the flower, we will grieve not, rather find the strength in what remains behind."

In the wake of my father's first stroke, our family faced a period of profound adjustment. The dynamics that once defined our household had shifted, and as we found our footing in a new reality, our father's indomitable spirit remained a guiding light. Despite his challenges, he continued to forge ahead, determined to contribute to our family's wellbeing. This chapter reflects on the moments that followed his strokes, the challenges we faced as a family, and the remarkable strength that emerged from those trying times.

From my mother's diary as written:

"After the untimely death of my beloved husband, on November 1,1968. I began to face the most difficult challenges.

1. To feed, clothe, and educate until they get degrees.

2. To give them help, guidance, or any kind of assistance so that they will live in the right direction, of course, with the divine love, "God's faithful love which is beyond comparison."

The untimely passing of my beloved husband marked the beginning of a chapter in my life that was defined by challenges. As I turned to the pages of my mother's diary, her words echoed with the weight of her responsibilities and the unwavering love she had for her family.

In her words, "After the untimely death of my beloved husband," she acknowledged the immense hurdles that lay ahead and the powerful force that would guide her through it all, God's faithful love.

Facing Financial Hurdles:

The loss of my father meant more than just an emotional blow; it was a financial earthquake that shook the very foundations of our family. The responsibility to feed, clothe, and educate my siblings and me fell squarely on my mother's shoulders. She embraced this responsibility with determination, seeking ways to provide despite the financial constraints. Through her efforts, we never lacked the essentials, a testament to her resourcefulness and unyielding commitment. This determination to provide for her children, even in the face of heartache, was a testament to her strength.

Guidance and Support

The diary entries revealed more than just sorrow; they revealed a heart that, while fractured, was resilient. "To give them help, the guidance of any kind of assistance so that they live in the right direction." Her words spoke of a mother's enduring love, a love that transcended loss and adversity.

My mother knew that financial support alone wouldn't suffice. With unwavering devotion, she made it her mission to provide us with guidance and assistance in every aspect of life. Her diary reveals her yearning to help us navigate the complexities of growing up, offering her wisdom as a compass. The depth of her concern is evident in her words. Every decision she made was driven by her desire to steer us towards a brighter future.

God's Faithful Love:

Amidst all the challenges, there was an underlying force that fortified my mother's spirit's unshakable faith in God's faithful love. It was this love that empowered her to face each day with resilience and optimism. "God's faithful love, which is beyond comparison," was the source of comfort, reminding her that she wasn't alone on this journey. This faith became her rock, enabling her to withstand the storms that life had hurled her way.

As I reflect on my mother's words, I am reminded of her unwavering strength in the face of adversity. Her journey was marked by sacrifice, determination, and an unbreakable bond with her family. In the chapters that followed my father's passing, her actions spoke louder than words, exemplifying the profound love she held for us. With "God's faithful love" as her guiding light, she managed the challenges with grace, leaving behind a legacy of resilience that continues to inspire us today.

The Void That Never Fades: Coping with Love:

"The saddest time in my life is during and after the death of my beloved partner." as written in her diary.

In the pages of my mother's diary, her emotions were laid bare, capturing the profound sorrow that had enveloped her world during and after the untimely death of her beloved partner. The weight of this loss was unlike any other she had experienced; it was a pain that lingered and echoed through every aspect of her life.

"The saddest time in my life," as she wrote, her words etched with the rawness of grief, "is during and after the death of my beloved partner." Each sentence seemed to echo the emptiness she felt, the void that could never truly be filled. In those moments, her pen became an outlet for the torrent of emotions that threatened to overwhelm her.

Gone was the presence that had been a constant in her life, the anchor that provided both guidance and companionship. The world seemed a little colder, a little lonelier without him by her side. She reflected on the shared dreams they had nurtured, the plans they had made, and the future that had once felt so certain. In his absence, those dreams remained suspended in time, forever incomplete.

The diary, filled with her thoughts and emotions, became a private sanctuary where she could pour out her heartache. It became a testament to her journey through grief, a journey that ultimately led her to find strength in her love for her family and her unwavering trust in a High Power.

In the end, her diary was not just a collection of words; it was a chronicle of resilience, love, and the unyielding spirit of a woman who weathered the storm of loss with grace and courage.

A Shared Sorrow: A Unified Strength

In the wake of our father's passing, our hearts were left shattered, each fragment carrying the weight of a profound loss that seemed to echo in the silence of our home. The pain of his absence was a heaviness we all bore, a heaviness that seemed to grow with each passing day. We were united by our broken hearts, bound together in grief that defied words but connected us in ways only deep sorrow can.

As we gathered around our mother, we became the pillars of support, the silent strength that she leaned on in the grace of her own profound loss. Each of us shared in the pain the void that his absence had left behind. We were no longer just siblings. We were a united front, a family bound by a common sorrow that transformed us into caregivers, confidants, and companions for our mother.

In the midst of her grief, our mother shouldered a burden that was not hers alone. She stepped into the role of both mother and father, embracing the challenges and responsibilities with a grace that was both inspiring and heartbreaking. Her sacrifices were evident in every act of love and care, every decision she made for our collective well-being.

In her diary, our mother's words reflected her deep gratitude for our presence and our unity in the face of adversity. She marveled at the resilience we exhibited, a testament to the love that bound us as a family. We may have been young, still navigating our own dreams and aspirations, but in that moment, we were warriors, steadfast in our commitment to stand by her side.

Amidst the profound sorrow that enveloped our hearts, the community gathered at the town municipal hall to bid farewell to my father, a man who had touched the lives of so many. As the #1 town councilor, his legacy of service and his warm presence resonated with all who knew him. The eulogy that echoed through the hall captured the essence of his life's dedication, and the multitude of attendees was a testament to the impact he had made on our town. It was a bittersweet moment, honoring a man whose memory will forever remain intertwined with the fabric of our community.

In the days, weeks, and months that followed, we embraced our roles with fierce determination. Our broken hearts, though heavy, were infused with a renewed sense of purpose. Our unity became a beacon of light in the darkness, a reminder that even in our deepest sorrows, we were never truly alone. As we navigated this new reality, we clung to the memory of our father's love, drawing strength from the legacy he left behind.

Chapter 16
A Mother's Love, A Daughter's Care:
Facing Challenges After Loss

"Resilience is not about never experiencing difficulties, but rather about how we respond and recover from them" -Sharon Salzburg.

In the somber aftermath of my father's passing, a new chapter of challenges and sacrifices unfolded for my mother and me. The weight of responsibilities fell heavily upon her shoulders as she navigated the uncharted waters of single parenthood while coping with the immense loss. In those poignant days, a bond of unwavering strength emerged between us as I stepped into a role I had never imagined-caregiver and protector during the final moments of my father's life. As I reflect upon those poignant times, I'm reminded of the sacrifices my mother made and the profound impact they had on our family's journey. This chapter is a testament to the resilience, love, and sacrifices that defined that pivotal period of our lives.'

"Journey of Love: Care and Compassion in the Midst of Loss"

In the midst of the bustling hospital corridors and the whirlwind of our individual pursuits, fate had cast us into a role we never imagined. It was a time when my siblings and I were at different stages of our educational journeys, each of us navigating the stormy waters of exams, lectures, and aspirations. And yet, life's unexpected turn had other plans for us. It was during my senior year in nursing school that destiny dealt its card, and I found myself at a crossroads of duty and devotion between my father's fading breaths and my own dreams.

As I juggled the complexities of my studies, the anticipation of graduation, and the demands of being a supportive sibling, a profound challenge emerged. My father's health deteriorated rapidly, and he was admitted to the very hospital where I was training. Amid the familiar hallways, I found myself straddling two worlds: the professional one, where I was becoming a nurse, and the deeply personal one, after my nursing classes and duty, where I was a caretaker for the man who had raised me.

In the midst of our family's challenging journey, a guiding light emerged in the form of a dear friend who was a part of our close-knit group of friends during my nursing years. As fate would have it, Dr. Rosendo Pacia, a dedicated medical intern at that time, crossed our path. He not only navigated the medical management with skill but also extended a hand of compassion and support to us. Amid his demanding duties at the hospital, he often found time to check on my father's condition and offer his insights to our family. His presence was reassuring during those trying days, and his willingness to step beyond the role of a medical intern to provide emotional support and medical expertise meant the world to us.

In those moments, I grappled with the duality of life and death, of the future and the past, converging with the confines of a hospital room. The walls witnessed my tears and my prayers, and the hospital bed held not only my father but also the embodiment of our family's journey.

As I walked the line between a devoted daughter and a budding nurse, I felt the weight of an education and a life in the balance. It was a chapter that blurred the lines between my identity, my aspirations, and the ties that bound us as a family. As my father took his last breaths, I understood that the education I had received went beyond textbooks and lectures; it was a lesson in compassion, resilience, and the profound connection between life, death, and the moments in between.

Unwavering Sacrifices: Navigating a New Path Alone

As the somber echoes of my father's passing lingered, a heavy cloak of responsibility descended upon my mother's shoulders. The sudden absence of the man who had been not only our father but also a pillar of our family left a void that was beyond measure. My mother, now in her fifties, stood at the crossroads of a new life, her journey as a widow fraught with challenges that would test her limits and redefine the very essence of her being.

In the wake of her beloved partner's departure, my mother was thrust into a role she hadn't anticipated- the sole provider and guardian for her 12 children. With four professionals, three college students, and the five younger ones still in need of education, the weight of financial responsibilities was staggering, yet my mother's determination remained unshaken.

She embarked on a relentless pursuit to secure our future, even if it meant sacrificing her own comfort and security. With teachers' wages as her only source of income, she navigated the complexities of budgeting, borrowing from banks, and even turning to loan sharks during tuition times. The land, once a symbol of our family's stability, was sold off piece by piece to fuel our education.

Amidst the tide of financial adversity, my mother clung to her unyielding hope that her children's education would be the beacon that guided us out of the darkness. Even as her own needs took a backseat, she resolved to empower us with the gift of education a legacy far more valuable than material wealth.

The upcoming months held a glimmer of promise as I neared the end of my nursing education. With graduation on the horizon, I felt a surge of determination to join my siblings in lightening the load that came to rest on my mother's shoulders. As I prepared to embark on my career, my heart ached for my younger brother Emiliano, who had just started his own nursing journey. The weight of his tuition costs weighed heavily, and my mother's perseverance in the face of financial turmoil was a testament to the strength of her love.

As I stood on the cusp of becoming a nurse, I understood that my role as a provider and a source of support was now intertwined with my mother's sacrifices. Together, we would navigate a new chapter of life, upholding the values my parents have instilled in us- unity, resilience, and unwavering commitment to family.

Facing Financial Realities

Senior year was meant to be a time of celebration and anticipation, a culmination of years of hard work and dedication. But as my brother embarked on his first year of nursing, we were acutely aware of the financial burdens that came with our aspirations. The passing of our father had reshaped the landscape of our family's financial stability, and the weight of our responsibility was felt more keenly than ever.

As we were in our nursing internship, my brother and I understood the magnitude of our financial responsibilities. With our mother working tirelessly to provide for our family, the expenses of our education seemed to grow exponentially. We navigated the reality of tuition fees, textbooks, and living expenses, all while trying to remain focused on our studies and clinical rotations.

Balancing Education and Commitments

The demands of nursing school were unrelenting, and as we faced the rigorous curriculum, we also carried the weight of our family's expectations. Our commitment to our studies had to be balanced with our responsibility to support our mother and younger siblings. Our dreams of becoming registered nurses were intertwined with our determination to honor our father's memory by achieving the success he had always envisioned for us.

Looking back, I see that our nursing years were a period of growth, resilience, and unity. We learned that while the weight of financial responsibilities could be heavy, the power of family and shared purpose was stronger. The challenges we faced together only fortified our determination to succeed, not just for ourselves but for our entire family.

As my brother navigated our years of nursing school, we carried the legacy of our father's resilience and our mother's sacrifices. The lessons we learned during this pivotal year would shape our paths in ways we could have never imagined.

In this chapter, we'll delve into the intricate tapestry of my mother's sacrifices, unveiling the layers of strength, love, and unbreakable determination that wove together to carry us through the toughest times.

CHAPTER 17
BORROWING HOPE: BUILDING DREAMS

"Most of the important things in the world have been accomplished by the people who have kept on trying when there seemed to be no hope at all."

Amidst the shadows of grief and uncertainty, my mother stood in the pillar of our family, determined to nurture hope in the hearts of her children. My father's untimely departure left a void not only in our home but also in our pursuit of education. At that time, my brother was on the cusp of his nursing journey, and I was preparing for my own graduation while another sibling was eagerly awaiting the start of college. The rest of the siblings were still navigating the tumultuous waters of high school.

In this chapter, we delve into the incredible determination and sacrifices made by our mother during the most challenging times of our family's life. Her unwavering commitment to ensuring her children's education, even if it meant seeking help from the most unlikely sources, paints a vivid picture of her resilience and love.

A Mother's Sacrifices: Juggling Finances to Secure Our Future

In the heart of our mother's indomitable spirit lay an unwavering commitment to our education, a commitment that would push her to extraordinary lengths. As I delve into the pages of her remarkable journey, I am drawn to a chapter filled with both hope and hardship. It's a chapter that speaks of a mother's unyielding love and determination.

Section 1: Borrowing from Loan Sharks

In the quiet corners of our home, where the walls bore witness to whispered prayers and the sacrifices etched into our existence, our mother wove a tapestry of resilience. The education of her twelve children was her paramount concern, and she bore the weight of that responsibility with unwavering grace.

To finance our dreams, our mother embarked on a journey of financial acrobatics that left us all astounded. She ventured into a world where loan sharks prowled like vultures, exploiting the desperate and the hopeful. With the regularity of her teacher's paycheck, she became a steady patron of these clandestine lenders. Her checks and my sister's checks, already meager, were sliced to silvers as they became both lifelines and shackles, ensuring our education but also perpetuating a cycle of debt.

In those challenging times, as education was the beacon of hope in our family, my mother, ever resilient and determined, sought ways to ensure that her children received the education they deserved. It was a difficult decision, one that she knew would cause some resentment and frustration among us, especially my sister. She made the selfless choice of using my sister Evangeline's paycheck as collateral for loans to cover our tuition fees.

This decision weighed heavy on my sister's heart, and her understandable resentment cast a shadow on our family. But my mother, driven by her unwavering commitment to our education, never wavered in her pursuit of our brighter future.

Section 2: Using Her Land as Collateral

It wasn't just the murky waters of informal lending; she also faced towering walls of financial institutions, offering her ancestral land as collateral. The plot of land, our ancestral heritage, became a bargaining chip in her unwavering pursuit of our dreams. It was a stark reminder that every diploma, every graduation cap, bore not just the sweat and toil of her children but also the sacrifices etched into that piece of earth.

Section 3: The Art of Frugality

In our family's life, my mother wove threads of frugality and practicality so seamlessly that they became an inseparable part of our existence.

In her world, there was no room for extravagance. She was the guardian of our resources, stretching every peso as if it were made of elastic, ensuring that it served its purpose efficiently. Her meticulous budgeting was a testament to her commitment to our education, a dedication that knew no bounds.

Clothes, for instance, were a luxury we rarely indulged in. If our attire was still serviceable and presentable, there was no need to squander money on the frivolity of new garments. Even my mother, the guardian of our thrift, hesitated to invest in her own wardrobe. She would jest about the scarcity of her purchases, sharing that even a new set of underwear was a rarity.

During my nursing internship, my brother and I felt the weight of her financial acumen. We didn't enjoy the typical weekend outings like our peers, as our pockets were void of allowances. But we didn't mind, for we understood that every peso saved was another investment in our education. The dormitory became our sanctuary, providing shelter and sustenance, and we were content.

My mother's unwavering commitment to frugality, though sometimes austere, was a testament to her love. She showed us that true wealth is not in material possessions but in the treasures of knowledge and opportunities. Her sacrifices were the threads that wove our family's story, binding us together on a journey toward a brighter future.

In the darkest hours of financial despair, our mother's sacrifices shone like a beacon of hope. She taught us that the pursuit of knowledge was worth every sacrifice and that dreams could be built even upon the foundations of debt.

In the end, my mother's sacrifices were not just financial transactions or acts of desperation. They were profound expressions of love, determination, and unwavering faith in the promise of a better future for her children. She understood that life's journey often requires navigation of rocky terrain, but she faced each challenge with courage that inspired us all.

Through her relentless pursuit, she taught us the value of resilience and the importance of family bonds. Her willingness to part with her cherished land was a testament to her belief that the dreams of one were the dreams of all. Our family's unity was unbreakable, forged through the fires of hardship and tested by the trials of life.

In the chapters that follow, I will continue to share the remarkable journey of my indomitable mother. Her sacrifices were the cornerstone of our family's achievements, and her faith and resilience continue to inspire us all.

CHAPTER 18
TALES OF RESILIENCE: A MOTHER'S UNWAVERING SUPPORT

"Patience is not simply not the ability to wait. It's about how we behave while we're waiting" -Joyce Meyer.

In the midst of adversity, my mother remained steadfast, and her unwavering resolve defined her legacy. Her sacrifices were the foundation upon which our futures were built, and her story serves as a timeless reminder that love knows no bounds and that a mother's love like hers is boundless.

Section 1: Waiting in Hope: A Mother's Patience

As a testimony of my older sisters Jerry and Evangeline, who were part of our mother's lending journey as their paychecks were also used as collateral in making loans, they witnessed our mother's patience in obtaining the much-needed loans. My younger sisters, Mona Liza, and Judith Leila, remembered vividly the extraordinary lengths to which our mother went to secure the funds that would fuel our dreams. Those long and arduous trips to people we knew only as lenders- individuals who held the keys to our education. It was a journey that left an indelible mark on their tender hearts.

They spoke of journeys that began before dawn, the first light of day breaking as they boarded overcrowded buses that meandered through winding roads. The journey, although routine, was fraught with uncertainty.

As they arrived at the humble abodes of these lenders, my sisters felt the weight of invisibility. They would sit for hours as if they did not exist. It was a test of patience and endurance, both for my mother and my sisters.

One of my sisters, Mona Liza, who was still very young, recalled those trying moments with remarkable clarity. "It felt as if we do not exist.", she would say, her voice carrying the wisdom that comes from witnessing a mother's determination. But amid the stifling wait, they also witnessed something extraordinary- a mother's unwavering resolve.

My mother's patience was a testament to her love, a love so fierce that it could weather even the longest days and the harsh judgements. She refused to give in to the despair that lingered in the air, her determination like a beacon that lit our path.

Those moments, sitting in the shadows of adulthood, had an impact far beyond their years. They learned that perseverance, even in the face of indifference, could move mountains. They understood that love could transcend the waiting and make each sacrifice worthwhile.

In the stories of our younger siblings, we find the strength that carried us through challenging times. Their memories, though etched in the innocence of childhood, illuminate the profound love and determination that defined our mother. These were the experiences that shaped us and taught us the true meaning of resilience and love.

Section 2: Enduring Love: A Mother's 3 AM Journey

In the labyrinth of life's challenges, there are moments that shimmer with an enduring love that leaves an indelible mark on our hearts. It was during my brother Emiliano's second year of nursing school that such a moment etched itself into the fabric of our family's story. It was a tale of determination, sacrifice, and a mother's unwavering devotion that unfolded in the early hours of dawn.

Anecdote:

Amid the hustle of nursing school, my brother found himself facing a seemingly insurmountable obstacle- the weight of unpaid tuition fees. It was a fateful day when his teacher delivered the crushing news that he wouldn't be allowed to take his exam due to his pending tuition fees. Dejected and disheartened, he retreated to his quarters, the weight of disappointment settling heavily upon him and thinking his pursuit of a nursing career was over.

An evening descended; the sting of frustration gnawed at my brother's heart. In a moment of despair, he sought refuge in the bottom of a glass with his roommate, drowning his sorrows in a haze of intoxication. But it was the light of the next day that would illuminate the depth of our mother's love and the lengths she would go to ensure her children's dreams remained intact.

It was a crisp morning, a moment frozen in time at 6 a.m., when my brother's life took a sharp turn. Through bleary eyes, he witnessed a taxi pulling up outside his residence. To his surprise, the figure that emerged was one other than our mother.

As she reached my brother's doorstep, breathless from her early morning odyssey, she held in her hands more than just a tuition payment. She clutched the threads of hope, determination, and unwavering commitment to her children's dreams. With a gaze that held a mother's love deeper than any ocean, she uttered the words that would mend my brother's heart, "I got your tuition."

In that instant, the fog of disappointment lifted, replaced by an awe-inspiring clarity. Our mother's act of love was a testament to her unyielding support. A beacon that cuts through the darkness of doubt. With the weight of financial constraints cast aside, my brother was granted a second chance- a special test that allowed him to prove his worth beyond the confines of unpaid fees.

In this chapter, we delve into this anecdote, a tale that exemplifies the depth of a mother's love, a love that transcends time zones and obstacles. It is a narrative that speaks of sacrifices made before sunrise, of a mother's willingness to journey into the unknown, all in the name of nurturing her children's dreams.

CHAPTER 19
NAVIGATING NEW PATHS

"Sacrificing for your family is a small price to pay for the joy and love they bring into your life" Unknown.

This chapter recounts the early years of my nursing career, filled with both professional growth and personal sacrifice. It serves as a testament to the enduring bonds of family and the indomitable spirit of my mother, who was unwavering in her commitment to securing a brighter future for her children.

Section 1: Professional Growth: Personal Sacrifice

Graduation day had finally arrived, and the proud moment of donning my nursing cap and pinning my badge signified not only the culmination of years of hard work but also marked a significant turning point in our family's journey. It was a bittersweet occasion, for just 6 months prior, we had bid farewell to our beloved father.

His absence loomed large, but the path forward beckoned, and I was determined to seize the opportunities that lay ahead.

With my nursing diploma in hand, I embarked on a new chapter of my life. The training hospital that had been my educational haven welcomed me as a full-fledged member of the Surgery Nursing Staff. The familial corridors and the scent of antiseptic became a second home. It was a comfort to be in the place where I trained my skills and forged lifelong friendships. However, life had changed irrevocably and I was now part of the family's financial support.

As fate would have it, my younger brother, Emiliano, was following in my footsteps, just beginning his own journey through the demanding world of nursing education. His dream of becoming a nurse was our family's beacon of hope. My mother, a pillar of unwavering determination, faced the financial challenge with remarkable resilience. She utilized my paycheck to support my brother's tuition and extended her assistance to our other siblings who were diligently pursuing their college degrees. This was the reality I willingly accepted: a life of financial responsibility mingled with the satisfaction of contributing to the future of my siblings.

Though my friends and co-workers often extended invitations for outings and leisurely escapades, I found myself restrained from budgetary issues. My meager earnings were not for fun and leisure but for fulfilling the aspirations of our family. Yet, amid the financial constraints, my friendships provided a source of solace. These friends, most of whom hailed from more privileged backgrounds, understood my situation and offered unwavering support.

In the midst of these challenges, I bore no resentment toward my mother. She navigated the financial intricacies of our family with grace and determination, making every effort to ensure that my brother and I could pursue our dreams. As the burdens of our family's education fell upon her shoulders, she stood resolute, a beacon of strength and selflessness.

Section 2: A Ring of Sacrifice and Love (Anecdote)

As graduation day for my brother drew near, there was one thing he desired more than anything else- a class ring. It was a symbol of his hard-earned achievement and a tangible reminder of his journey through nursing school. But the reality of our family's financial situation at that time weighed heavily on my mother's shoulders.

During one of her visits to my brother, he mustered the courage to ask her for the money needed to purchase the coveted class ring. However, the response he received was not what he had expected. My mother, with her characteristic honesty and unwavering love, told him that she simply didn't have the funds.

The cost of the ring, 250.00 pesos, seemed beyond reach. My brother, disappointed and frustrated, couldn't help but express his concerns. He was worried about the embarrassment of being the only one without a class ring, especially on such an important occasion as graduation day. The prospect of facing his classmates without this symbol of accomplishment weighed heavily on his mind.

Yet, something remarkable happened in the following weeks. Despite her own financial constraints, my mother found a way to fulfill her son's desire. She realized that the money she had set aside for her own needs, specifically for her dentures, could be postponed. With a heart full of love and sacrifice, she handed my brother the 250 pesos he needed for his class ring.

For my brother, this act of selflessness was a profound demonstration of my mother's unwavering support and love. She willingly put her own needs on hold to ensure her child's happiness and pride on his graduation day. The ring my brother wore wasn't just a piece of jewelry; it was a symbol of the sacrifices my mother made for her children, and it served as a constant reminder of her boundless love.

In this poignant moment, my mother's choice to delay her own needs for the sake of her child's happiness epitomized the essence of her motherhood. It was a testament to her enduring love and her willingness to go to great lengths to ensure her children's dreams and aspirations were realized.

This anecdote serves as a timeless reminder of the sacrifices made by mothers all around the world who, in the face of their own challenges, find a way to give their children the world.

Section 4: A Mother's Determined Role (Anecdote)

As the opportunity for my brother to work in the United States drew near, a mixture of excitement and anxiety filled our household. While we were all proud of his accomplishment, the reality of the financial burden weighed heavily on our shoulders. It was my mother, our unwavering matriarch, who took it upon herself to navigate this challenge.

One sunny morning, with a sense of determination that mirrored her unyielding spirit, she handed my brother a small piece of paper. On it were written two names, two hopes for a brighter future. They were names that resonated with influence and affluence in our small community.

With that note in hand, my brother embarked on a journey of visits, conversations, and expectations. The first destination, home of a distant relative known for their wealth, filled with hope. But hope, as it sometimes does, gave way to disappointment as his plea for financial support fell on deaf ears.

Undeterred, my mother had already devised a backup plan. She presented him with another note, directing him to another prominent figure in our community. This time, the weight of our family's dreams and aspirations rested on the shoulders of this meeting.

Yet again, destiny has its own plans. The second attempt proved futile. But my mother, an ever-resilient soul, wasn't disheartened. She knew that sometimes, life's most significant achievements were born from tenacity.

With an unshakeable belief in the power of family, my mother chose an alternative path. She sold a portion of her beloved land to my sister Evangeline, who was already established in her own life. Together, they constructed a new home adjacent to ours, not only securing my brother's future but also strengthening the bonds that held our family together.

At that moment, my mother's sacrifice was clear. She was not just providing financial support; she was symbolizing the very essence of our family's resilience. This chapter of our lives was yet another testament to her unwavering love and resourcefulness.

CHAPTER 20
SUPPORTING THE NEXT GENERATION

"Learning is a lifetime journey. Growing older merely adds experience to knowledge and wisdom to curiosity."

In the midst of life's challenges and transitions, a new chapter unfolded, one that would test the limits of our family's strength and resilience. It began with the day I proudly received my nursing degree, six months after my father's passing. With my diploma in hand and a nursing job secured, I entered a new phase of my life, one where I would become a pillar of support for my family, particularly my younger siblings.

As the years rolled on and I established my career as a nurse, our family dynamics evolved. My two older sisters and older brother had embarked on their own journeys, with marriages and new families of their own. The transition placed a new set of responsibilities on my shoulders.

As I continued to help my mother support my brother's tuition in nursing, my younger brothers pursued their dreams of higher education, striving for degrees in various fields. The weight of tuition fees and living expenses pressed heavily on my mother's shoulders. She had already weathered countless storms, always finding a way to ensure that education remained our guiding light.

However, even as we held onto this hope, there were still three siblings in high school, attending Catholic school (newly opened in our town with high standards and excellent reputation) that required financial resources we didn't have in abundance. But my family's determination was unwavering.

During this period, my living situation played a crucial role. While I enjoyed free housing and my brother resided in the dormitories, it was a blessing that allowed us to redirect funds where they were needed most. My older sister Thelma stepped in and provided a helping hand to our brothers, offering them a place to stay during their college years.

This rotation of support became our way of life, a testament to the strength of our familial bonds.

In this evolving tapestry of love and sacrifice, we understood that education was the key to a bright future. As each sibling found their footing in life, we collectively shouldered the responsibility of ensuring the next generation could walk the same path toward success.

Navigating Uncertain Waters

In the wake of our family's financial struggle, with two nursing college tuitions looming on the horizon, my mother made a difficult decision regarding my brother Fred's future. She believed that taking a year off from school would serve two important purposes: alleviate the financial burden on our family and allow Fred to mature away from the influences of alcohol that had started to creep into his life.

Fred's Journey:

This is a story of my brother Fred's remarkable and inspiring tale of determination and hard work. Taking a year off from school, my brother Fred decided with my mother's approval, to work for my aunt and uncle in Tayasan, a coastal municipality in the province of Negros Oriental, Philippines. The island is across Cebu Island. They owned multiple businesses where my brother was welcomed as a family. According to the memories of his wife, as was told by Fred, he started working in the gas station, then he worked on the plantation and learned how to drive a tractor. During his work, he learned how to drive a vehicle while working in our aunt and uncle's business endeavors. He was enjoying his stay with our cousins while acquiring skills and experiences during his year of working, and he personally grew more mature.

Fred's Path to Success:

Following the year of self-discovery and hard labor, my brother Fred's aspirations to pursue higher education burned brighter than ever. This section chronicles his unwavering commitment to obtaining a college degree amidst our family's financial struggle.

Through his dedication and commitment to pursue college, he returned home potentially more mature and with a new perspective. He applied as a working student at the University of San Carlos. He starts working at dawn as a janitor. He had to clean and wax corridors before class started, and when nobody was at the university before he went to classes like a normal student. He was also serving as an altar boy in the university chapel and eventually rising to the position of Librarian at the main university library.

As he was a working student, he had free lodging at my sister's place. My sister Thelma's memory of Fred was that he did all the laundry while he was staying with her, left home for work at dawn, and gave him a small allowance.

Fred managed his time and studies during these challenging times. His work and study had made a positive impact on his academic achievement.

He graduated with a Bachelor of Science in Commerce, majoring in accounting, with flying colors.

From his working student years to his educational triumph, Fred's journey began his professional career when he secured a job in a prominent shipping company called "Aboitiz Shipping."

In the tapestry of our family's journey, Fred's story is a testament to the power of determination and the profound love that binds us together. With unwavering commitment, he embraced the role of a working student, transforming early mornings as a janitor and diligent hours in the library into stepping stones toward his dreams. It was a year of pause that enabled him to leap forward.

But Fred's story isn't just about his individual struggle. It is a testament to the values that run through our family's veins. Our mother's instinct and sacrifice, her financial prudence, and her relentless determination paved the way for Fred's education. She knew that by giving him time and opportunity, he could spread his wings and, in doing so, lessen her burden.

The story wouldn't be complete without my sister Thelma's pivotal role, providing him shelter and a small allowance. It's a testament to teamwork within our family. In unity, we thrive. In each other's sacrifice, we find strength.

Fred's journey wasn't merely about him but about us all. It was a collective effort to ensure that every sibling received the gift of education. In this chapter, the spirit of our family reflects the tenacity of our mother's dream. Through trials and triumphs, our family remained resilient, and together we crafted a brighter future.

Alex's Colorful and Diverse Educational Journey:

Throughout his life, our beloved brother embarked on an extraordinary journey that showcased his remarkable adaptability and unwavering determination. He initially set his sights on a career in healthcare, starting with what our mother remembered during her video interview with her grandchildren. Alex did not pursue his nursing internship but discovered his new passion and graduated with a Bachelor of Fisheries in Carigara, a hidden gem in the northern part of Leyte in the Philippines. Passed the board exam with flying colors. Eventually, he shared his expertise as a dedicated teacher in a distant city.

But his journey did not stop there. Drawn by a thirst for new experience, he ventured to Saudi Arabia, broadening his horizons and adding an international perspective to his diverse skills. Upon returning to our hometown, he briefly rested before discovering his passion for excelling in embalming courses, eventually becoming a top-tier professional and managing a reputable mortuary corporation.

His desire to serve his community led him to yet another path. He became a dedicated Barangay councilor in our cherished town of Moalboal, where he used his wisdom and compassion to make a lasting impact on the lives of those he served. His remarkable journey reflects a man of incredible versatility, passion, and commitment.

This chapter, like the others, is a thread in the tapestry of our family's memoir- a memoir of sacrifices, resilience, and unwavering faith in the power of education. It is a testament to our mother's vision and the commitment of each sibling to ensure her dream becomes a reality. Our family, united in purpose, emerged from these trials stronger, closer, and even more deeply connected.

CHAPTER 21
GUIDING THE NEXT GENERATION: A SHARED JOURNEY

"There is no one road to success; There are as many as there are people willing to build them"

In the unfolding pages of our family's story, the torch of education now passed into the hands of the last three siblings. Their journey through higher learning, marked by dedication and resilience, brought new challenges and triumphs into our lives. This chapter delves into their pursuit of knowledge, their unwavering commitment, and how our family continued to stand together to ensure their successes. As we navigate the final leg of this educational odyssey, the bonds that hold us become even more profound, revealing the true strength of our unity.

As years unfolded, a unique arrangement emerged. My younger brother, armed with his own freshly earned nursing degrees, set his sights on opportunities abroad, eventually securing a job in the United States. His journey mirrored mine in many ways, yet it marked a turning point in our family's narrative. With me as their anchor, my siblings could venture into the city for college without the financial burden of housing expenses.

Section 1: Continuing the Journey; Pursuing My Bachelor's Degree in Nursing

As the years passed and my nursing career unfolded, I found myself at a crossroads. Armed with my Registered Nurse degree, I had already embarked on a fulfilling journey of caring for my patients and supporting my family. Deep within me, there was a thirst for knowledge and a desire to reach new heights in my profession. It was this drive that led me to make the decision to continue my education, pursuing a Bachelor's Degree in Nursing. The path ahead was daunting, as it required a delicate balance between my professional duties, my commitment to my family, and the pursuit of my own dreams.

To achieve this balance, I enrolled in evening classes. These were challenging times, with late-night study sessions, exams to prepare for, and assignments to complete. However, I was driven by a sense of purpose and desire to grow professionally, provide even better care to my patients, and set an example for my younger siblings.

As I embarked on my journey to attain a higher degree in nursing, I continued to help my mother support my brothers' education. The torch of responsibility had been passed to my younger brothers. I couldn't help but be there for them, just as my older siblings had been there for me.

The pursuit of my Bachelor's degree in Nursing was a challenging chapter in my life.

Section 2: After Marriage: A Unified Family

Marriage marked a new chapter in my life, but it didn't alter my commitment to my family. Instead, it expanded the circle of those I was determined to help. Our humble city dwelling became a sanctuary for my younger brother, Francz, and younger sisters, Mona Liza and Judith Leila, during their college years. In those shared spaces, we discovered the true meaning of family bonds. My younger siblings remained by my side as they pursued their education, and they became an integral part of my own growing family. They were almost second parents to my children. Little did

I know, these years would not only shape their futures but strengthen our bond as a family.

My mother, who was relieved from the burden of housing finances, also received financial support from my brother Emiliano in the US and my brother Fred's contribution for my younger sibling's tuition fees. My sister Mona Liza, as a working student in college, eased my mother's burden of tuition fees. Together, we navigated the challenges, embraced the joys, and forged an unbreakable bond that went beyond blood ties.

In the tapestry of our family's educational journey, my three younger siblings wove some of the most vibrant threads. While the challenges they faced were formidable, their determination shone like a beacon. Together, my younger siblings not only secured their degrees but also ventured into a professional world, adding their unique brilliance to our family's constellation of success.

Section 3: Francz: Educational Journey

Among the vibrant tapestry of our family's educational pursuits, there was always one thread that remained understated and quietly resilient. The thread belonged to our youngest brother, whose journey to college and into the professional world was marked by a calm determination and an admirable sense of privacy.

While the rest of us shared our academic triumphs and challenges, our younger brother preferred to work diligently behind the scenes. We often wondered at his ability to maintain an aura of mystery around his college years and career, only later to discover that he had graduated with a Bachelor of Science in Business Administration.

In his own way, he had carved his path, choosing to remain humble about his achievements. After graduation, he embarked on a career in the world of security and operations planning, a choice that reflected his quiet strength and dedication to his responsibilities.

His story reminds us that not all journeys are loud and flamboyant; some are marked by a steadfast resolve to excel and contribute in one's own unique way. As we reflect on our family's educational tapestry, we recognize that his quiet perseverance is an integral part of our shared narrative, adding depth and diversity to the fabric of our lives.

Section 4: Mona Liza's Academic Success

In the midst of our family's journey through financial hardships, my sister, Mona Liza, emerged as a beacon of determination and academic excellence. She embarked on her college journey with unwavering resolve, not only as a student but also as a working scholar.

While many might have succumbed to the pressures of such a demanding path, Mona Liza excelled. Her commitment to her studies was nothing short of inspirational. She spent long hours in both the classroom and her part-time job, never allowing exhaustion to deter her from her goals.

As the years passed, her dedication bore fruit. She didn't just graduate but did so with flying colors earning the prestigious title of Magna Cum Laude. Her achievement was a testament to her unwavering spirit and the indomitable willpower that runs in our family. My sister had shown us that with determination and hard work, even the most challenging circumstances could be overcome. After her graduation, she secured a job at United Coconut Planters Bank in a managerial position.

Her story reminds us that education is a powerful tool, one that can elevate us above our circumstances and set us on a path toward success. Mona Liza proved that regardless of the obstacles life may throw our way, with the right mindset and unyielding perseverance, we can achieve greatness.

Section 5: Judith Leila's Challenges of Education and Love

In the tapestry of our family's education-driven saga, the thread of our youngest sister's story is vibrant and unique. Like a graceful dancer on the stage of life, she twirled her way through the challenges of academia and love, guided by the watchful eyes of our indomitable mother.

As my sister, Judith, ventured into her college years, the allure of a budding romance started to encircle her world. Like any teenager, she was navigating the complex terrain of youthful infatuation. However, my mother, with her unwavering focus on education, was determined that matters of her heart would not compromise my sister's path to success.

Throughout her college years, our mother's watchful eye never wavered; she knew the value of an education and the importance of a strong foundation for her youngest child.

She would keep a close eye on my sister's activities, and though it might have seemed strict at times, her intentions were clear -education first.

While love and the allure of romance beckoned on the horizon, our sister remained committed to completing her studies. She chose to major in Bachelor of Science in Education, with a focus on Physical Education, a testament to her love for movement and vitality.

Graduation day marked the end of one chapter and the beginning of another. Our sister had earned her degree, but love had also found its way into her heart. A year after donning her academic regalia vows and embarking on a new adventure-marriage. It was a testament to our mother's dream: to see each of her children not only educated but also happy and settled in life.

Our youngest sister's journey was a testament to the power of education and the love of a family that was willing to make sacrifices to ensure she succeeded.

The story that unfolds is one of dedication, resourcefulness, and love. It's a testament to the unbreakable bonds of family and the lengths we were willing to go to ensure the next generation receives the opportunities they deserve. As I look back on those years, I am reminded that support comes in many forms, and the sacrifices made during that chapter of our lives were worth every penny and every moment.

As we reflect on the triumphant odyssey of my three younger siblings through academia and into the world of work, we are reminded that the pursuit of knowledge and the relentless pursuit of one's dreams are at the heart of our family's story. Their achievements illuminate the path for generations to come, affirming that with resilience and unwavering support, even the loftiest of goals can be reached.

CHAPTER 22
A NEW DAWN: EMBRACING LIFE'S ADVENTURES

"Life is either a daring adventure or nothing at all."

By Helen Keller

As the final chapter of her teaching career closed, a new chapter of adventure and explorations opened up in my mother's life. Her life had been an unending cycle of early morning lesson plans and nurturing young minds. After dedicating 42 years to educating 12 children, witnessing them achieve their dreams and secure their futures, she found herself standing at the threshold of a new era.

Retirement was not merely an end to a long career; it was a well-earned respite from the daily hustle and bustle of teaching and ensuring that her children received the best education possible. It was time to pause, reflect, and enjoy the fruits of her labor.

Retirement was not just a milestone; it was a ticket to a world she had only dreamt of- a world of leisure, travel, and long-awaited visits to families and relatives both far and near.

In this chapter, we delve into the moments that defined her transition into retirement. It is the story of a remarkable woman who, even in her newfound freedom, continued to inspire us with her unwavering dedication to family and community. As she adjusted to a quieter life, she found that her journey was far from over. It was simply taking a different path.

Section 1: Living with Purpose; Faith and Community

In the serene years following her retirement, my mother embraced a new chapter of her life with unwavering enthusiasm. Freed from the demands of her teaching career and the responsibilities of raising a dozen children, she found solace and purpose in her deep-rooted faith. Her days were no longer constrained by the school bell or the bustling household. Instead, she dedicated her time to her beloved "Sagrado Corazon de Jesus" group, where her unwavering devotion radiated through her every action.

As if by divine calling, she became a beacon of light in our local chapel, "San Roque." Her leadership skills, honed through decades of nurturing her family, took a new form. She assumed the role of president, leading the congregation with grace and humility. Under her guidance, the small chapel flourished as she tirelessly organized fundraisers and community events to improve the infrastructure. To her, this was not just about bricks and mortar; it was about creating a sacred space where hearts could find solace, and spirits could be uplifted.

Her retirement was marked by camaraderie and spiritual fulfillment. The bonds she forged with fellow worshippers and friends in the community grew stronger, a testament to her warm and nurturing personality. She had discovered that life after retirement was not merely a conclusion but a vibrant continuation. In her newfound freedom, she thrived, her radiant smile reflecting the contentment she found in her spiritual and social endeavors.

Section 2: Evenings of Cards and Lottery Luck,

After her well-deserved retirement, my mother's life took a delightful turn. With her trusted companion, Marichu Gabato, she embraced leisure in its simplest forms. Evenings often saw them engrossed in spirited games of "Tung-it," a local card game akin to Gin Rummy. Money changed hands, laughter filled the room, and for my mother, it was a cherished routine that brightened her days.

My mother's fascination with numbers persisted. She meticulously tracks her own set of digits, chasing the elusive thrill of the lottery. Her numbers were not random; they were drawn from everyday life, etched into her memory like the price tags of the products she'd encountered during the shopping spree to the city. In her retirement, she found a way to keep her mind agile and engaged.

Section 3: Baking Bliss and Boundless Generosity

But perhaps one of the sweetest moments of her post-retirement life was found in her love for baking. Her kitchen transformed into a haven of aromas as she crafted cakes and goodies, especially cookies. I am so amazed watching her bake with ease and so organized in her measuring ingredients. She has a recipe book that she treasures so much. We learned a lot from her cooking and as a teacher and mother, she made sure all of us knew how to cook and bake. Cooking, especially baking, was an enduring passion that filled her heart with joy. My children look forward to her cookies when they come home from school, at the time when she was living with me. The irresistible scent of freshly baked treats became synonymous with her presence.

While she maintained a sense of financial discipline, as her long-time caregiver and companion attests, she possessed a heart of boundless generosity. My mother was the steadfast pillar of support for anyone in need. She offered financial aid to those facing hardship and a helping hand to struggling neighbors. She never forgot a birthday, always showering her friends with thoughtful gifts.

Section 4: Mahjong Moments: Laughter and "Otap" with Auntie Moning

In the warm afternoons of her retirement, my mother found joy in an unexpected past-teaching the younger generation how to play mahjong, with a sparkle in her eyes, she patiently instructed our young relative, Joy S. Abad, in the art of the game. As the ivory tile clicked together in symphony, my mother's wisdom mingled with the innocent curiosity of youth.

In those moments of play and camaraderie, laughter filled the room. It was a chorus of merriment that knew no age boundaries, bridging the gap between generations. After each victorious round, my mother would reward her pupils with a pack of "otap", the beloved Filipino crackers, as a token of her affection.

Joy, who was often at the receiving end of both mahjong lessons and snacks later remarked, "Their laughter was the best medicine." It was these simple, shared moments that my mother found immeasurable joy in the twilight of her retirement.

Section 5. Finding Joy in Retirement Through TV

Retirement offered my mother the gift of time, a precious commodity she had often sacrificed in her busy years. Now the one-time extremely busy woman who had traversed the world to provide for her family had the luxury to sit back and savor the simple pleasures of life. Her eyes twinkled with delight as she delved in her favorite shows, mostly rerun of old movies and some Filipino drama shows.

But her interests didn't end there, she was also captivated by the art of baking, to the baking show that aired. The intricate designs of cakes and pastries fascinated her and she took up her own culinary adventures in the kitchen, filling our home with the scent of freshly baked goods.

In her desire to stay connected with the world, CNN was her portal to international news. Even in her tranquil retirement, she kept a watchful eye on the events unfolding around the globe. When she heard about the U.S. recession, she couldn't contain her curiosity. With a hint of concern in her voice, she'd call me and ask, "What happened to America? Is it going to be poor? It's supposed to be the richest country". She tried to keep abreast of current events in the U.S. where some of her siblings have their residence abroad.

These shows provided more than just entertainment, they were the bridge between her life as a working mother and her peaceful retirement. They were her escape, her source of laughter, and her cherished moments in the company of beloved fictional characters. Retirement brought her the time to relish these simple yet significant joys.

This chapter of her life was a tapestry of newfound freedoms, enduring kindness, and the artistry of the kitchen. It reflected her unwavering commitment to both simple pleasures and the well-being of those around her.

CHAPTER 23
JOURNEY BEYOND BORDERS

"Life begins at the end of your comfort zone."

-Neale Donald Walsh

In the early 1980s, a new chapter in our family's journey was about to unfold. After years of hard work, dedication, and helping my younger siblings in their education journey, I received an opportunity that would not only shape my own future but would also pave the way for a significant turning point in our family's life. It was in the year 1980 when I secured employment in the United States, a momentous achievement that carried with it the promise of better prospects and the realization of long-cherished dreams. This opportunity marked the beginning of a new adventure, one that would eventually reunite our family under a single roof in a foreign land.

In the chapters that detail my mother's travels, I'll weave in the inspirations she drew from us, myself, and my brother Emiliano Jr., who are already in the United States in the lovely state of California in pursuit of our dreams. The narrative will illustrate how our resilience and determination from the USA fueled her own yearning for new horizons. With our stories as a backdrop, my mother's adventures in the USA become not only a personal exploration but also a testament to the unbreakable bonds of family and the profound impact one generation can have on the next. It's a reminder that dreams, when shared and nurtured within a loving family, can transcend borders and generations, inspiring each member to reach the stars.

Section 1: Setting Foot in a New World

In the quiet corners of our home, amidst shelves adorned with family photographs and cherished mementos, my mother kept a treasure trove of memories. They have meticulously documented journeys, each with its unique story, destinations, and emotions.

Her most prized possession was a simple diary with vibrant recollections of her adventures. Each entry was a testament to her attention to detail. Dates, port of entry, itineraries, and names of her companions were all there.

As I leafed through the pages, I could almost hear her voice narrating the tales of her journeys. She did not just document the sights and sounds; she recorded her emotions - the thrill of stepping onto foreign soil, the warmth of reconnecting with family and friends, the homesickness that occasionally crept in, and the immense joy of experiencing the world.

In her meticulous records, she left us a legacy of wanderlust and wonder, a reminder that life's greatest treasures are often found not in possessions but in the memories we create. And for that, we are eternally grateful.

Section 1: Setting Foot in A New World

In the twilight of her life, my mother embarked on a remarkable odyssey that took her far beyond the boundaries of her homeland. Her quest wasn't for treasure or fame but rather a deeper understanding of the world and a desire to embrace the experiences it offered. It was a journey that both enriched her soul and allowed her to share her indomitable spirit with people from diverse corners of the globe. As I recount her travels, I'll take you on a captivating voyage filled with fascinating encounters, unforgettable landscapes, and the enduring lessons she carried back home. This is a story of my mother's wanderlust, a wanderlust that knew no age, no boundaries, and no limits.

July 26, 1984-April 12, 1985 (Seattle - Port of Entry)
Destination: California

As written in her diary, one of her favorite memories was her first trip to California, USA, in 1984.

"As the day of departure approached, my heart danced with excitement and trepidation. The prospect of traveling to the United States, a land I had only heard of in tales and seen in pictures, filled me with an exhilarating mix of emotions. My bags were packed with care, filled not just with clothes and essentials but with dreams and aspirations. Yet, as I stood at the airport, surrounded by the hustle and bustle of travelers and the echoing announcements of flights, a shiver of fear ran down my spine. I was about to embark on a journey of over 14 hours, crossing oceans and continents all alone.

Yet, in that moment of doubt, I clung to my dreams, for they were the beacons guiding me through the stormy seas of uncertainty. With my family's love and blessing in heart, I took a deep breath and boarded that plane, ready to embrace the unknown. Little did I know that this voyage would not only take me to a distant land but would also lead me to new friendships, adventures, and a chapter in my life that would forever change me."

Section 2: A New Beginning in the USA

In the summer of July 1984, the long-anticipated moment arrived. My mother, a retired teacher and a seasoned traveler within her homeland, embarked on a journey that will redefine her life- her first visit to the United States. With a heart filled with excitement, she stepped off the plane onto foreign soil, a land of dreams and opportunities.

Her destination was my brother's home, where the warm embrace of family awaited her. Our household was bustling with life with my own family. Three energetic children, Karla (9), Jerome (8), and John Paul (6), made sure there was never a dull moment. Among them was my youngest son, who faced his own unique challenge: adapting to the American education system.

For my mother, the transition into this new chapter of her life was seamless. Her role as a retired teacher resurfaced with grace and pose. She became both a mother and a teacher once again. Patiently, she guided my youngest son, John Paul, who was entering school for the very first time.

Flashcards filled our living room, each one adorned with the fundamentals of reading and writing. My mother dedicated herself to instilling these skills in her young grandchild. Day after day, she watched as his understanding of the English alphabet blossomed. She cherished every small victory as if it were a golden moment, knowing that she was playing a vital role in her grandson's growth.

In addition to her tutoring duties, my mother also extended her nurturing care to a family friend's daughter, Roxanne, providing a safe haven for this young child in our home. Her time was split between teaching, babysitting, and sharing stories of her own homeland.

Section 3: The Sweet Aromas of Love

Among the many delights of Mama's stay in the US was her cherished role as a family's resident chef and baker. She would often surprise her grandchildren with the irresistible aroma of freshly baked cookies when they returned from school. The kitchen became a place of enchantment as they watched her skillfully create their favorite treats, crafting a special bond with such a delicious batch.

As the afternoon sun spilled into the kitchen, her warm smile mirrored the golden-brown cookies. The clinging of mixing bowls and the sweet scent of vanilla enveloped the room as she shared her culinary secrets with the eager young audience. Every cookie had a story, a secret ingredient, and a dash of love.

To her grandchildren, these cookies were more than just baked goods. They were tokens of affection, offering comfort after a long school day and a tangible reminder that their Lola was always there to nurture both their bodies and hearts.

Even in this foreign land, she managed to create an atmosphere that was unmistakably a Filipino blend of warmth, hospitality, and, of course, delicious home-cooked meals.

Section 4: TV Tunes

During her first visit to the United States, my mother found solace in the warmth of our home while we, her children, were away at work and the grandchildren at school. In the midst of those quiet moments, she discovered a new world through the television. Her favorites were the classic comedies 'I Love Lucy" and "Three Is a Company." But it wasn't just laughter that captivated her; she had a fascination with car racing and would watch races with intensity as if cheering on her favorite driver.

Moreover, Mama was drawn to "The Oprah Winfrey Show." The inspirational stories and discussion on this show seemed to resonate deeply with her. But it wasn't just entertainment; Mama valued knowledge, especially when it came to health and nutrition. She would absorb every piece of advice, making mental notes of the tips and recommendations. This newfound knowledge about nutrition became her guide to a healthy lifestyle, one she continued to follow even when she returned to the Philippines. It was as if she had adopted these lessons as a lifelong commitment to wellbeing.

Through the television screen, my mother was not only entertained but educated. It was a reflection of her desire to stay engaged, learn, and adopt positive practices in her life.

Section 5: Weekend Discoveries: First Impressions in the USA

In the early days of her maiden voyage to the United States, the weekend held a special magic for my mother. With the anticipation that was infectious, she looked forward to our family outings, her eyes filled with wonder at the opportunities this new land had to offer.

On Saturdays and Sundays, when my brother and I were off from work, the world became our oyster. No longer confined by the mundane, she was eager to explore the unfamiliar. Every outing was a voyage of discovery, and she savored every moment of it.

Parks, with their lush greenery and the simple joy of family picnics, became treasured destinations. In these open spaces, she witnessed the laughter and the boundless energy of her grandchildren as they ran and played. The exuberance of youth blended harmoniously with the calm contemplation of age.

Dining out at the diverse array of restaurants in this foreign land offered her a taste of new cultures and traditions. Each meal was an adventure in culinary exploration, and she marveled at the different flavors and the varied backgrounds of those who prepared the food.

But it was the malls, those enormous meccas of American consumerism, that left her truly awestruck. In her homeland, the idea of a mall was relatively small-scale compared to these sprawling retail wonders. She couldn't get enough of the vast spaces, and the Thanksgiving and Christmas decorations, with their grandeur and sheer opulence, filled her heart with the spirit of the season.

This weekend outings, where she witnessed the beauty of nature, savored the tastes of diverse cultures, and bathed in the radiant glow of holiday decorations, were like pages ripped from her travelogue of dreams. They enrich her first visit to the US with unforgettable moments and a sense of fulfillment. She reveled in these family moments, excited and happy in togetherness that transcended geographical borders.

These were her moments of adventure and discovery, where she could explore the new and unfamiliar.

This journey was just the beginning of a series of visits, six in all, that would define her relationship with the United States. But this first trip was unique, as it introduced her to the American way of celebrating Thanksgiving and Christmas. The traditions and festivities were unlike anything she had ever experienced back home. Yet she embraced them with open arms. Thanksgiving dinners, with their abundance of dishes and heartfelt gratitude, filled her heart with warmth. The magic of her first American Christmas, with its sparkling lights, beautifully adorned trees, and the joy of giving, left an indelible mark on her.

Through this chapter of her life, my mother discovered that home wasn't just a place on a map; it was wherever family and love resided. With each day that passed, her heart swelled with pride for her family's achievements in the land of opportunity. Her stay in the US became more than a journey- it became a testament to the enduring bonds of family and the unwavering spirit of a mother.

As we reflect on this inaugural visit, we are reminded that it was just the first chapter in a series of adventures yet to unfold. My mother's story in America would span decades, encompassing countless more travels, celebrations, and challenges. Each visit brought with it unique experiences, joys, and even lessons.

In the chapters that follow, we'll embark on a remarkable journey through Mama's many visits to the U.S., exploring the moments of joy and connection as well as the trials she faced with her indomitable spirit.

So, as we bid adieu to this first visit, let us look forward to turning the pages of her life story in America. The chapters that follow will reveal the incredible tapestry of her experiences, and we'll witness how each visit added new colors to the canvas of her life. Through it all, she remained steadfast, proving that no distance is too great and no obstacle too challenging when love and determination light the way.

CHAPTER 24
ADVENTURES ACROSS THE OCEAN: MY MOTHER'S U.S. VISITS

"Only those who risk going too far can possibly find out how far they can go"-T.S.

Section 1: Mother's Second Visit: April 16, 1986- January 14,1987.

(L.A. Ca. Port of Entry)

In the warmth of another year's arrival, my mother embarked on her second journey to the land of dreams and opportunities- the United States. This time, her heart was filled not only with anticipation but also with the excitement of a joyous occasion, my brother Emiliano's wedding to her beautiful bride, Genevieve Gobuyan. She was accompanied by my two sisters, Thelma and Mona Liza, and a cherished cousin, Preciosa, all eager to witness the union of our family with newfound family ties.

As she stepped onto American soil once more, her senses were greeted with the familiar scents and sounds of this foreign yet strangely welcoming land. It was a reunion with both her loved ones and the newfound friends she had made during her previous visit.

On her second visit my mother's journey was filled with new beginnings and joyous celebrations. This time, she stayed at my brother's place, where the atmosphere was brimming with excitement as wedding preparations were in full swing.

The wedding celebration exceeded her expectations, leaving her heart aglow with happiness. It was her experience of a Filipino wedding on American soil, where the vibrant traditions of her homeland were seamlessly intertwined with the customs of her new surroundings.

During her stay, my mother embarked on exciting adventures. She explored the enchanting world of Disneyland with my two sisters. Hollywood's iconic landmarks also beckoned to her, and she marveled at the glamor of the entertainment.

The highlight of this voyage was undoubtedly my brother's wedding, a culmination of love and commitment that had begun with my mother's gracious request for her hand in marriage. However, the festivities were not confined to a single day. Every moment in this journey, my mother embraced with the same fervor she had brought to her initial adventure.

Accompanied by my sisters, her journey in the land of opportunities was not just about festivities but also about bonding and creating precious memories.

My sister Mona Liza had to fly back home after a three-month visit, while my mother flew back home with Thelma and Preciosa after seven seven-month stay.

The trip was a testament to the bonds of family and the beauty of experiencing life's milestones together. It was another chapter in her American adventure, filled with love, laughter, and the promise of an even more remarkable journey.

Section 2: Third Visit to the USA: A Year of Gatherings and Adventures

July 13, 1988-August 28, 1989 (L.A. Port of Entry)

In the summer of 1988, Mama embarked on her journey to the United States, eager to reunite with her children and explore new adventures. Little did she know that her visit would turn into a year filled with family gatherings, unexpected reunions, and exciting explorations.

A. Arrival of Thelma and Nene (family friend) (November 1987) On November 1, 1987, just before Mama's third visit, her daughter, Thelma and a close family friend, Nene, landed in the United States. They shared housing under my roof for a few months before they ventured out on their own, searching for job opportunities and independence in this foreign land.

B. Mama's Arrival (July 1988)

Then, on July 13, 1988, Mama and my sister Jerry arrived who briefly stayed with my brother and his family in Southern California, her heart bringing with anticipation. Her mission was clear: to reconnect with her children and create cherished memories together. Her arrival marked the beginning of a series of memorable family gatherings. She lived with me during the rest of her stay in the US.

C. Mona Liza Joins the Reunion (February 11, 1989)

The family reunion didn't stop there. In February 1989, my sister Mona Liza, also made her journey to the U.S. She also lived with me in Northern California. The family was now partially complete, and the stage was set for the year of togetherness.

D. Adventures and Explorations:

During Mama's third visit to the U.S the entire family was in for an unforgettable time filled with joy, adventure, and a touch of Lady Luck. The visit stretched from July 13, 1988 to August 28, 1989, making a chapter of unforgettable memories.

First and foremost, the trip was a season of celebrations, especially for my children. Each of their birthdays became a grand occasion. The house resonated with laughter as we hosted vibrant birthday parties, complete with delicious cakes and gleeful squares of youngsters.

One particular adventure that stands out is our visit to Las Vegas. It was Mama's first encounter with the glittering lights and vibrant energy of a casino. Her excitement was palpable as she tried her luck at the slot machines, and her joy was infectious as we watched the roulette wheel spin. Even though we didn't win big, the experience left us with cherished memories and a few tokens as souvenirs.

Of course, the holiday season was a magical time. Mama's presence added a warm and loving touch to our Christmas and New Year celebrations. The house was adorned with twinkling lights and festive decorations. Mama's culinary skills shone once again as she prepared a feast. Family and friends gathered, sharing laughter, stories, and the spirit of togetherness.

While her third visit presented significant challenges for me, I found myself raising my children on my own, and during this time, my mother displayed an unprecedented level of unwavering love and support. Yet my mother was there by my side, providing not just emotional strength but also a helping hand whenever it was needed. Her presence during this time was a testament to her enduring love and the depths of her maternal care.

This chapter of Mama's travel diaries was a time of festivities, adventures, and her first encounter with the allure of the casino world. But most importantly, it was a testament to the enduring bond of family and the love that knows no distance.

Section 3: Mother's Fourth Visit to the U.S.A.

December 3, 1991- December 4, 1992, San Francisco, Port of Entry

A. Seasons of Celebration: Mama's Stay in Pleasanton

During my mother's fourth visit to the United States, her stay was extended for a year. By this time, I had my own home in Pleasanton, California, a place of relative calm amid the tempestuous teenage years of my children, who were 13, 14, and 16. While I was at work, Mama took charge of the household, providing nourishing meals and delicious baked goods. However, the phase of adolescence was not without challenges.

As teenagers often do, my kids had their share of quarrels and disputes. These moments sometimes left Mama feeling anxious and worried as she listened to their disagreements and occasional physical fights. Yet, as every devoted mother and grandmother, she persevered, keeping the family fed and cared for.

On the fourth visit, which coincided with the festive holiday season, my mother found herself swept up with the Thanksgiving, Christmas, and New Year's celebrations. These gatherings were not just about the traditions we held dear but also an opportunity for her to witness the bustling merriment and warm bonds within the family.

During Mama's 4th visit to the US, our family established some cherished holiday traditions that added an extra layer of warmth and joy to our celebrations. Christmas, in particular, was a remarkable time. We had this beautiful tradition of gathering at our friend Marcie Muneses's place in Pleasanton. The house would be adorned with sparkling lights and vibrant decorations, and the air would be filled with the heartwarming aroma of Christmas delicacies.

Our family and dear friends would come together under one roof, creating an atmosphere brimming with love and togetherness. Mama was at the heart of it all, her eyes glowing with happiness as she watched her children and grandchildren engage in laughter, stories, and, of course, the grand tradition of gift-giving. Those moments were etched in our memories as the true essence of family bonds.

But the festivities did not end there. As Christmas turned into New Year, it was my turn to host the grand celebration. Our home in Pleasanton became a hub of excitement and anticipation. We would decorate the house in preparation for the big party, ensuring that it sparkled with festive lights, streamers, and an array of delicious food and treats. Enjoyed singing karaoke and dancing all night. It was a labor of love, and it was always worthwhile to see the smiles on everyone's faces as they gathered to welcome the New Year.

These gatherings were not just revelry; they were about reaffirming the bonds that held our family and friends together. There were moments when we celebrated life, love, and the hope for a bright future, and Mama was right at the heart of it all, radiating happiness and love, cherishing each and every moment.

Thanksgiving brought the aroma of a grand feast, where the whole family gathered around a lavishly adorned table. My mother marveled at the diverse array of dishes, from the golden roasted turkey to her favorite cranberry sauce. The hearty laughter and stories shared around the table seemed to weave an invisible thread connecting our family and special family friends.

B. *Exploring Alexandria: A Journey through History (1992)*

During my mother's fourth visit to the U.S., she embarked on a memorable journey to Alexandria, Virginia. Her spirit of adventure led her to explore new horizons, visiting her sister-in-law Bebing in the charming town of Oxon Hill, Maryland. During her stay in the heart of history-rich Alexandria, she had the opportunity to immerse herself in the vibrant past of this iconic city. Guided by our dear cousin Vellie, she traversed the cobbled streets and iconic landmarks that echoed stories of America's yesteryears. This visit, filled with both nostalgia and curiosity, etched yet another chapter of exploration in her remarkable life.

C. The Long Wait; Mama's Path to US Residency

This year, my mother's visit to the U.S. also coincided with an important period of waiting. We were eagerly anticipating the approval and interview for her permanent residence, a process we had initiated nearly four years prior. As the months passed, our hopes grew, and Mama's presence in our home became a symbol of the enduring bond of family and the promise of a brighter future together.

In the warmth of American summer as the years unfolded. My mother embarked on a journey that bridged borders and reunited our hearts. Her fourth visit to the United States was marked not only by cherished moments with her grandchildren but also by a family reunion that will forever remain in our memory.

As she bade farewell to the comforts of our home, she left behind the echoes of laughter, the aroma of her culinary creations, and the indomitable spirit of a mother who tirelessly nurtured her family. Her absence was palpable, but her love and influence transcended the oceans that separated us. In the years that followed, her life would be filled with more adventures, more travels, and more love shared with her children, grandchildren, and great-grandchildren.

D. Choosing Home over Opportunity

In 1992, after years of meticulous paperwork and a waiting game with immigration, the moment finally arrived. We received a letter confirming that my mother's application for permanent residency had been approved. It was a triumph, a dream fulfilled after years of patience and hard work.

The letter contained a schedule for an interview at the embassy, a crucial step toward obtaining her green card. But life has a way of presenting choices, sometimes ones we least expect. My mother was already in the United States when this golden opportunity arose. Her heart longed to return to our homeland, to the familiar streets, faces, and the warmth of her community. She knew the interview was important, a chance for a more secure future, yet she also knew that her heart was rooted in the place she had always called home.

In a decision that may have seemed baffling to some, my mother made a choice that was entirely hers. She declined the interview, writing a heartfelt letter to the immigration explaining the situation. It wasn't a decision she took lightly, and it wasn't about turning away from opportunities. It was about the pull of her roots, the love of her family and her hometown, and the comfort of her familiar surroundings.

Some might say she had a chance of a lifetime, and they wouldn't be wrong. But what she found in that choice was something equally invaluable: the freedom to live life on her own terms. She chose to be where her heart felt the most joy, where her roots ran the deepest. It wasn't about rejecting an opportunity; it was about embracing the life she loved and the people who mattered most.

In that moment, my mother taught us that life isn't just about chasing the biggest opportunities; it's also about cherishing the ones we already have. Above all, it's making choices that align with our hearts, our deepest desires, and the love we hold for the people and places that make life truly meaningful.

I often find myself pondering what might have been if my mother had chosen to accept the offer of permanent residency in the United States. The decision to decline the interview and return to her hometown was a choice that shaped the course of our family's life. This "what if" scenario lingers in my thoughts, like an alternate reality we can only wonder. What opportunities might have unfolded? What challenges would we have faced? The road not taken is the path filled with questions and possibilities, and I can't help but reflect on the unique journey that we've embarked upon due to her decision.

CHAPTER 25
THE LEGACY OF LOVE: THE EMMO SANDALO
REUNION

June 30-July 5, 1995

"In family life, love is the oil that eases friction, the cement that binds closer together, and the music that brings harmony." - Friedrich Nietzsche

This chapter delves into the heartwarming story of the EMMO Sandalo Grand Reunion, a five-day extravaganza that brought together families from far and wide to honor our greatest treasure-our mother.

This reunion, named after our beloved parents, Emiliano and Monica, was not just a gathering of relatives; it was a tribute to a remarkable mother who had poured her heart and soul into raising her twelve children. This was a celebration of Monica, the

Matriarch of the Sandalo clan, who had faced life's challenges with resilience and a smile and who had been a source of inspiration for her children scattered across the globe.

Let's dive into the unforgettable journey of love, laughter, and the ties that bind, as we explore the details of the EMMO Sandalo Reunion, a celebration of family, heritage, and the legacy of a remarkable woman, Monica Babiera Sandalo.

Activities of our Grand Reunion:

June 30, 1995- Family Meeting and Pasalubong Distribution

On this day, only the 12 children gathered for a family meeting. It was a moment of pure family bonding as we discussed various matters, shared stories, and finalized the details of the reunion event. The highlight of the day was the distribution of gifts (Pasalubong) from family members abroad, filled with love and warmth.

July 1, 1995- Formal Grand Reunion at Cebu Plaza Hotel

This was the main event, the culmination of our family reunion. In the heart of Cebu City, beneath the grand chandeliers of the prestigious hotel, a momentous event was about to unfold. As the doors of the grand ballroom swung open, the stage was set for a reunion like no other- the EMMO Sandalo Reunion. The occasion was no ordinary family gathering; it was the culmination of years of planning, love, and unwavering bond that tied the Sandalo family together. It was a night of glamour and celebration. We came together dressed in our finest attire, ready to honor our beloved mother. Speeches, tributes, and heartfelt messages filled the air. Special guests, close relatives, and friends joined us for a memorable evening.

A Memorable Evening at Cebu Plaza Hotel

On July 1, 1995, a date etched in our family's history, we gathered at the prestigious Cebu Plaza Hotel for the grandest family reunion we had ever organized. It was a night of joy, laughter, and heartfelt moments that still resonate with us to this day.

The evening commenced with an exquisite dinner prepared by the hotel's expert caterers. The aroma of delicious dishes filled the air as we took our seats, eager to celebrate not only our union but the matriarch who brought us all together, Mama.

The grand reunion was a celebration of the heart and it all began with a heartfelt prayer. The responsibility of invoking blessings upon our gathering fell upon the capable shoulders of Rev. Father Cholo Sungcad, a dear old family friend and neighbor from our hometown.

As the room filled with the murmurs of family conversations and the aroma of forthcoming dinner, Father Cholo stood before us. His familiar face was a reassuring sight, a connection to our roots. With a calm and gentle voice, he led us in a prayer that invoked blessings, gratitude, and a sense of unity.

His words resonated deeply with our shared faith, setting the tone for the evening's celebration. Through his words, we were reminded of the divine presence that had watched over our family throughout the years. It was a moment that brought together generations, comforting and guiding us with the wisdom of both our earthly bonds and our shared spirituality.

Father Cholo's invocation was more than just a prayer; it was a bridge between our past and our future. It marked the beginning of a memorable evening, one where love, laughter, and cherished moments flowed as freely as the blessings he invoked.

Our beloved late brother, Fred, the family comedian, took the stage for his words of welcome. His humor and wit had the entire room in stitches. His introduction set the tone for the evening, blending heartfelt sentiments with laughter.

Following his act, our eldest late brother Leo took the floor to offer his opening remarks. His words were a testament to the importance of family bonds, evoking nostalgia for shared moments that had brought us to this grand occasion.

As the first chords of "If We Hold On Together" filled the room, we sang together, united by the powerful message of the song. It was a poignant moment that reminded us of the strength in unity and our commitment to preserving our family's unique legacy.

The spotlight then shifted to our sister Mona Liza, who graced the stage with a touching tribute to Mama. Her words were a heartfelt expression of gratitude for the woman who had dedicated her life to nurturing and loving us.

One by one, each of Mama's twelve children, their spouses, and her adoring grandchildren stepped forward to present their gifts. These offerings represented the individuality of each family within our larger family tree, a testament to our deep connection to one another.

Mama's response was a culmination of love and appreciation, her eyes brimming with tears as she acknowledged the love that radiated from her family. Her heartfelt words touched our souls, reminding us that it was her strength and love that had made this reunion possible.

The night concluded with our family anthem, "The Greatest Love of All," a song that resonated deeply with our shared values and the enduring love within our family.

As the program concluded, the festivities continued with songs, dances, and lively games. Our dedicated master of ceremonies, Anthony Bucad and Amai Sandalo, guided us through the remainder of the evening, ensuring everyone was entertained.

The event reached its peak during the closing remarks, delivered by Bonnie Villanueva, a fitting closure to an evening that had united us all. Then, without further ado, the dance floor came to life as the night transitioned into a joyful celebration.

It was an unforgettable evening, an ode to family and togetherness, one that would remain etched in our hearts and memories,

As the night of our grand reunion unfolded, the atmosphere was electrified with excitement. The air was filled with laughter, chatter, and the sweet melodies of music that invited everyone to the dance floor. But what made this night truly special were the gifts we gave to our mother from each family, the speeches from my brothers, and the dancing presentations, a tradition that had become our signature as a Sandalo family. It was a night of celebrations, of connections renewed, and of a legacy of love that continued to flourish.

During this memorable event, our family was blessed to have some very special guests who graced the occasion. These esteemed relatives included my sister's brother, the honorable Atty. Luciano

Babiera and his wife, Mary. Also in attendance was my mother's cousin, Lucia (we call her Tia Lor) Araneta, along with her husband Ramon, Lucia's daughter Mildred, and her husband, the venerable Atty Pacianito Cabaron.

On my father's side, we were honored to have my uncle, Ernesto Sandalo, and his lovely wife, Elsie, as our cherished guests. Each of them added a touch of elegance to the gathering.

One of the most touching moments of the evening was the surprise speech delivered by our uncle, Atty. Luciano. He shared his immense joy and pride that we were celebrating and honoring our remarkable mother, his cherished sister. Deep in his heart, he even went as far as suggesting that my mother deserved a place in the local Cebu paper as the "Greatest Mother of All Times". His heartfelt words made the occasion even more special, and we were all profoundly thankful to have witnessed such a memorable gathering.

In looking back at our 1995 reunion, we are reminded that the special guests who graced the occasion, our dear relatives and friends, have since departed this world. Their presence during that unforgettable evening is etched into the tapestry of our family's history. Only Mildred, our dear cousin and a steadfast witness to our celebration, remains among us.

In the years that have passed, our hearts are heavy with the loss of loved ones. Their smiles, their laughter, and their endearing words are treasured memories. Among those who were with us, dear Tia Lor, with her eloquent prose, painted a vivid picture of that remarkable night in a heartfelt letter that spans three pages. In her writing, she shared her deep honor of being a part of our grand celebration, describing the event in meticulous details. Tia Lor's words provide a window into the past, allowing us to relive those cherished moments, and we are grateful for her beautiful recollection.

July 2-1995 Thanksgiving Mass and Cemetery Visit: (Moalboal)

A day of reflection and remembrance. We attended a Thanksgiving Mass to express our gratitude for our mother and all the blessings we've received.

Afterward, we visited the cemetery, paying respects to our departed loved ones, especially to our late father. It was a time of introspection and cherishing the memories we hold dear.

July 3- Beach Party and Ball Games

The reunion concluded with a day of fun and games. We headed to the beach for a vibrant beach party. Laughter, joy, and camaraderie filled the air as we played ball games and enjoyed the sun and sea. It was a perfect way to end our grand reunion with a splash of energy and unity.

As the "EMMO Sandalo Reunion" came to a close, it wasn't just the adults who had shared stories and laughter. The younger cousins, raised on different shores but bound by blood, had formed bonds that transcended geography.

They played together in the azure waters of the Moalboal beach, explored the familiar yet enchanting streets of Cebu City, and shared secrets beneath a starlit sky.

In the midst of tearful goodbyes, it became evident that the reunion had ignited a special connection among the younger generation. The cousins, once separated by oceans, had become confidants, allies, and friends. The partings were difficult, marked by heartfelt promises of reuniting again soon.

And so, the "EMMO Sandalo Reunion" accomplished something profound. It brought together a family, not just in celebration but in the forging of lasting bonds. As the younger cousins waved their goodbyes, their shared waves of laughter echoed in the air, a testament to the enduring strength of family ties. It was the reunion that Mama, the heart of the family, had cherished, and its legacy lived on through the warmth and camaraderie of the youngest generations.

The "EMMO Sandalo Reunion "was not just a tribute to our beloved Mama; it was a testament to the power of family to bridge, the miles strengthen connections, and create memories that would be cherished for generations to come.

On the grand day of our family reunion, amidst the grandeur and unity, it was our beloved Mama's turn to speak. Her words were a reflection of a heart full of gratitude and love for her children and their families. She expressed her feelings eloquently, capturing the essence of this monstrous occasion.

Excerpts from Mama's Speech:

"I thank the Lord for the privilege of giving us the grand affair to reunite my children and their children, knowing and seeing them happily and lovingly. I thank everybody for their thoughtfulness and great plans for this 1st Grand reunion. This made me very excited and happy that we are here together as one big family. I hope this occasion will be a memorable one for our children and generations to come. My short message for husbands and wives is "Honor thy father and mother."

In the wake of our Grand Family reunion in 1995, the memories continued to reverberate even across miles. My dear Aunt, who traveled to be a part of this momentous occasion, penned a heartfelt 3-page letter to express her profound sentiments. Her words painted a vivid picture of the event and the warmth she felt among our large, interconnected family. Though our paths had diverged, the bonds we shared persisted, and her letter was a poignant reminder of the love that transcended distance and time.

In her letter, she conveyed her immense gratitude for the invitation to the reunion and the opportunity for her family to witness the heartfelt joy and love that permeated the event. She was, alas, we all were, deeply touched by the shared experiences and rekindling of connections. Her letter became a testament to the enduring strength of family ties and the significance of this grand celebration in all our lives.

As I read her words, I was reminded of the vast tapestry of memories we were weaving and the lasting impact that this grand reunion had on all of us. It was a reminder that love and family endure, no matter the distances that may separate us.

Excerpts from Tia Lor's Letter to me in the US regarding the EMMO Sandalo Reunion:

In the heartfelt letter to me from my dear Aunt Tia Lor (actually our older cousin), who was one of the special guests during our grand reunion, she beautifully described Mama's emotions during the reunion. She wrote:

"Your affair at Plaza Hotel last July 1 was the best reunion I had ever witnessed. It wasn't merely a reunion but paying tribute to a beloved mother from her devoted children. It surely was unique. I believe that evening was one of the happiest memorable days of your mother's life. I, too, felt the same."

"Fred's words of wisdom were full of wit and humor, Leos' opening remarks gave the audience an idea why your mother deserves the honor of being the greatest mother of all. From emcees. Allan and Amai, Rev. Fr. Cholo's invocation, down to presentations (messages, songs, dances), Auntie Moning's

response and Bonnies closing remarks, everything was so wonderful. Orchids to you dears, for having thought of such an affair. Surely being the children of the greatest mother, you her children are also great yourselves, no wonder you are such grateful and affectionate children to your Mom"

Auntie, as she fondly calls my mother, has undergone a remarkable transformation since your visit and reunion. She now radiates happiness, in contrast to before when she appeared to carry a heavy burden. She exudes relaxation and constantly beams with joy. Your efforts and expenses in organizing this reunion and tribute to her were far from in vain; we are truly thankful for this positive change in her.

In the grand ballroom of the prestigious Cebu Plaza Hotel, under the sparkling chandeliers and amid a sea of loved ones, we gathered to honor a woman who had given us the world. The "EMMO Sandalo Reunion" had been a three-day crescendo of love and gratitude, but it was in this grand moment that the tears welled up in her eyes. She stood in the spotlight, not for her sake, but as the heart of our immense family. The plaque we presented engraved "The Greatest Mother"; it was not just an award but an embodiment of our collective affection. It was a moment that transcended words, an unspoken understanding of the depth of her influence. With tears in her eyes, she knew her legacy was secure in the love of her children, for it was not her name but her love that would echo through generations to come.

Legacy of Land: An Inheritance Shared

In anticipation of her grand reunion with her twelve children, she had already undertaken a significant task- dividing her land, the inheritance she had diligently preserved over the years. As she surveyed the land, numbered each parcel, and arranged a system for equitable distribution, my mother's determination was evident. She already anticipated that this would be the right moment when all her twelve children are in one place at the same time.

At the age of 77, my mother displayed a level of preparedness and foresight that was truly remarkable. My mother embarked on a profound journey, one that was deeply rooted in the cherished values of family and inheritance. It was an act of love and practicality, ensuring that her legacy would be securely placed in the hands of her children while she still had the strength to oversee it.

It was more than a simple division; it was an expression of her unwavering belief in preserving family heritage and a testament to her enduring commitment to ensure that her legacy would continue to thrive.

This act, a testament to her thoughtfulness, proactive approach, and her deep concern for our well-being, allowed her to find peace in the knowledge that her children's futures were secured.

CHAPTER 26
PHILIPPINE ODYSSEY: TACLOBAN/DAVAO TRIPS AND SEEKING INDEPENDENCE

"Home is not a place; it is wherever your family is."

In the tapestry of my mother's adventurous life, there were threads of wanderlust that spanned beyond international borders. In the heart of her beloved Philippines, my mother embarked on a series of journeys that would enkindle her connection with family and homeland.

These trips, made with a heart full of warmth, allowed her to traverse the archipelago's diverse landscapes and, most importantly, reunite with her cherished siblings and their families.

Section 1: Tacloban City (1986)

Tacloban is the capital city of the province of Leyte. It is the largest city and distributing center in the eastern Visayas Islands. During her trip to Tacloban, my mother had to experience riding a

Ferry that leaves from Cebu City to Leyte. As the boat gently rocked against the emerald waves, my mother would find herself in a peculiar state of tranquil anticipation. Her gaze, fixed upon the horizon where sea and sky converged, held a sense of wonder and calm. For in these moments, she wasn't just traversing the open sea; she was connecting dots of her life, bridging the gaps between family and friends, weaving stronger bonds with each nautical mile. The boat ride, often heralding reunions or joyous visits, was a unique tapestry of emotions- a patchwork of excitement, nostalgia, and the sheer beauty of the Philippines that she carried within her heart.

First, she ventured eastward to the picturesque city of Tacloban, where my sister, Evangeline, and her family had established their home. Amidst the coastal beauty and vibrant culture of Leyte, she savored moments of familial togetherness, creating lasting memories.

During her visit to Tacloban, my sister and her family played the role of gracious hosts and tour guides, taking my mother to some of Leyte's most iconic and historically significant places.

Together, they crossed the San Juanico Bridge, an engineering marvel connecting Leyte and Samar.

At MacArthur Park, they stood in awe of General Douglas MacArthur's monument, a tribute to his return to the Philippines during World War II.

Then, my mother marveled at the opulence of the Santo Nino Shrine, once owned by the infamous Imelda Marcus, showcasing its grandeur and artistry.

These trips not only immersed my mother in history but also allowed her to witness the vibrant culture of Leyte and bond with her adoring grandchildren, creating a tapestry of experience that would forever be etched in her heart.

Section 2: Davao (May 28, 1997- June 7, 1997)

My mother made her way southward to the bustling metropolis of Davao, where my brother Eddie's household awaited her arrival.

During her memorable journey to Davao, my mother's eyes were met with the lush landscapes and vibrant cityscape of the southern gem. She was welcomed into my brother Eddie's abode, where he had established his own business.

One sunny day, they strolled along the serene promenades of Magsaysay Park, with its picturesque view of Davao Gulf and the majestic Mount Apo in the backdrop. The park, a true reflection of the city's peaceful and harmonious atmosphere, left a lasting impression on her.

Determined to explore the heart of Davao City, they ventured into the bustling capital, immersing themselves in the local culture and vibrancy.

One of the highlights of her visit was a tour of the iconic Insular Hotel, where she marveled at the blend of modern elegance and traditional charm. The hotel stood as a testament to the city's rich history and its journey towards progress.

During her week-long stay, my mother cherished moments spent with her sister-in-law (my father's youngest sister), Aunt Corazon Aninon, and her family. The warmth and camaraderie that flowed between them were heartwarming, proving that family bonds can thrive across generations and distances.

In Davao, my mother experienced a fusion of nature's beauty, urban sophistication, and the love of her family. It was a week of cherished memories and new discoveries that would forever remain etched in her heart.

Furthermore, she embarked on a delightful journey to Puentispera Orchid Gallery, where vibrant blooms painted the landscape with riots of colors and fragrances.

Not only did she reconnect with family, but she also rekindled friendships with old companions. She reconnected with Atty. Sales and also visited Nancy Sebumpan. They dined together, sharing laughter and the stories of their journeys through life. These moments of togetherness were a testament to the enduring bonds of friendship that time and distance couldn't diminish.

In Davao, her journey continued as she embraced the charm of Mindanao, reconnecting with relatives and basking in the warm hospitality of my aunt's family. Through these travels, my mother found solace and renewed bonds, deepening the roots of her family tree in the fertile soil of her homeland.

Section 3: Seeking Independence: The Drive for her Transportation

In 1999, as my mother returned home from her adventurous trips to the United States and her trips in the Philippines, she found herself at a crossroads. At 81 years old, her spirit remained unyielding, but the physical toll of age was starting to affect her daily life. The bustling streets of Cebu City, once navigated with ease, were becoming a challenge. Stepping onto the crowded buses

192

was a daunting task, and long rides were an ordeal. Even the simplest of needs, like going to the bathroom during lengthy bus journeys, felt like insurmountable obstacles. She realized that to maintain her independence and continue her active life, it was time to seek her own transportation solution. This marked a new chapter where she would explore new roads of self-reliance, even at her seasoned age. She found herself longing for a more dignified mode of transportation, one that could cater to her specific needs.

It was during this time that she made a simple yet profound request to me- the acquisition of a car. With newfound freedom awaiting her, she envisaged a life of less worry, more convenience, and cherished bathroom breaks. I heeded her call, and the day she received her car marked a turning point in her life. No longer dependent on the uncertainties of public transit, she was met with the respect she rightfully deserved.

My mother was very proud of her "prized possession," She treated it with great care, making sure it was spotless, well-maintained, and cherished like a part of the family. She had it polished its exterior meticulously and proudly parked it in front of her home, a symbol of her independence.

However, her newfound freedom did not just revolve around having a car. It centered on the bond she nurtured with my late brother Fred, her steadfast companion and driver. Together, they embarked on daily adventures into the city, weaving through traffic with ease. In each outing, their connection grew stronger. They shared business deals, city escapades, and heartwarming meals at local restaurants, especially at the famous "Jollibee "restaurant.

The car, once a symbol of liberation, became a vessel of precious moments and companionship. It allowed my mother to explore not only the roads of Cebu City but also the depths of their bond. It was a chapter in her life when she could witness her desires realized and her connections strengthened, proving that even in the face of challenges, she continued to embrace life's opportunities.

CHAPTER 27
CONTINUING JOURNEYS AND FAMILY MILESTONES

"Take only memories, leave only footprints" -by Chief Seattle.

After several memorable journeys abroad, my mother's sense of adventure was still burning bright. At the young age of 78, she embarked on her fifth and sixth visits to the U.S., embracing the chance to reconnect with family, create new memories, and explore the diverse landscapes of the country she had grown to love. Little did we know these visits would coincide with a significant milestone in our family's history.

September 10, 1996 - April 11, 1997(Port of Entry- San Francisco)

During her fifth visit to the United States, my mother's journey was marked by adventure and exploration. She spent most of her time in Pleasanton, California, where I had settled with my family. Together, we embarked on memorable trips to some of California's most captivating destinations.

Yosemite National Park:

Our visit to Yosemite, a national park of California, was nothing short of awe- inspiring, an icon of America's majestic natural beauty. The majestic waterfalls, towering granite cliffs, and pristine wilderness left an indelible mark on my mother. She reveled in the sheer grandeur of nature, capturing its beauty in her heart.

Water World

A day of aquatic fun awaited us at the Water World, a park that delighted us with thrilling slides and rides. The joy on my mother's face as she splashed around with her grandchildren, was a testament to the happiness these moments brought her.

Carmel and Salinas

Our family connections extended to Salinas, where we visited our family friend Winnie Ellis and her family. It was a heartwarming reunion filled with shared stories and fond memories.

Nestled along the rugged coastline of California's central Coast, the 17-mile drive in Carmel is a breathtaking journey that promises natural beauty at every turn. As my family, dear mother, and our cherished friend embarked on the adventure, we were on an unforgettable day of exploration and awe- inspiring sights.

The drive began at the Iconic Pacific Grove, a gateway to a world of coastal wonders. Cypress Point Lookout was our final stop along the 17-mile drive. Hence, we stood in silence, gazing out at the vastness of the Pacific. My mother, her eyes reflecting the wisdom of her years, whispered that nature was the greatest artist of all. It was a day of connection, reflection, and deep appreciation for the wonders of our world.

San Diego

We embarked on an unforgettable road trip from Pleasanton to San Diego. The road stretched out before us like an endless ribbon of possibility, the Californian sun casting a warm glow on the highway. My mother, ever the adventurous spirit, sat comfortably in the back seat with our family friend Marcie Muneses while

Hillis was driving us safely on our road trip odyssey. We knew it would be a journey filled with exploration and cherished memories.

Our first stop on this road trip was at historic mission churches, a testament to California's rich and diverse history. Mission San Juan Capistrano, with its iconic bell tower, captivated us all. We wandered through the courtyards, imagining the lives of those who had walked these paths long before us. My mother was so captivated by the history of mission churches.

As we continued our journey southward, the anticipation of reaching San Diego grew. We had the pleasure of meeting our old friend, Ester, who was a resident of San Diego at that time. She took us to Old Town San Diego, a place where history comes alive in the form of adobe buildings, lively marketplaces, and street performers. My mother enjoyed the atmosphere, embracing the fusion of cultures and traditions that make California so unique. We had dinner, sipped drinks and enjoyed live music. We also ventured to Harbor Island, a place where the ocean breeze mingled with laughter and live music. My mother was enjoying every minute of our adventure.

Through every twist and turn of the road, my mother's eyes sparkled with wonder. This road trip was more than just a journey from one place to another; it was an adventure, an exploration of history and culture, and most importantly, a bonding experience that would forever bind our hearts.

Las Vegas

Our journey took a lively turn in Las Vegas, where my mother tried her luck at the casinos for the second time. She embraced the vibrant energy of the city and, true to her spirit, enjoyed the experience to the fullest.

Additionally, during this visit, my mother had the opportunity to stay with my brother in Camarillo for a week. This precious time allowed her to bond intimately with his family, creating cherished memories that would last a lifetime.

August 28, 1998- May 4, 1999 (Port of Entry- San Francisco)

During her 6th visit to the United States, my mother embarked on an adventure that would be etched in her memory forever. This

198

time, she stayed at my sister Mona Liza's home. From the west coast to the east, and even down south to Florida, she embraced every moment of her extended stay. It was a journey filled with family reunions, celebrations, and explorations of new places. In this chapter, we'll delve into exciting experiences that made this visit an unforgettable one for Mama.

Reno, Nevada Trip

My mother's eyes sparkled with excitement as she recounted her adventures in Reno. Not once, not twice, but thrice, she ventured into the glittering city of casinos and entertainment with my sister, Thelma, and a dear family friend, Nene. Her face lit up as she shared tales of lively nights spent in the slot machines, the thrill of trying her luck, and the camaraderie they all shared in the vibrant city. It was evident that these trips to Reno had etched unforgettable memories in her heart, where joy and laughter echoed through the dazzling lights of the casinos.

Tech Museum of Innovation in San Jose

Her journey began with an exploration of the high-tech wonders of Silicon Valley, a world so different from her humble beginnings. Yet, it was the simplicity of family dinners every Sunday that warmed her heart. No longer the cook on this special day but the cherished guest, she relished these moments. On other days, she loved cooking and baking for the family.

A Momentous Day: My Wedding (September 5, 1998.)

My mother graced my wedding to my groom, Hillis E. Golden, with her presence, adding her blessing to our new union held in Pleasanton, California. On that unforgettable day, my mother took center stage in a role of profound significance. It was an event that held a special significance for us because it marked the introduction of a cultural dimension into our family.

On the day of my wedding, as I stood there in anticipation, the moment arrived when the wedding march began to play. I looked toward the entrance, and there she was, my mother, arm with my beloved brother, Emiliano. The sight of her brought a profound sense of joy and pride that words alone could not describe.

My mother, at that moment, was the epitome of elegance. Dressed impeccably in an outfit that radiated her timeless elegance, she was the epitome of grace and sophistication. Her presence was a testament to her strength, her enduring love, and the pride she took in her family.

As they walked down the aisle together, it was a poignant reminder of the unbreakable bonds of our family. My mother's unwavering support, her beauty, and her poise were a source of inspiration. She was not just walking down the aisle, but she was also walking with me into the new chapter of life.

It was a moment filled with profound meaning and deep emotion, one that I will cherish. My mother's elegance and grace on that day were a reflection of the love and guidance she had always given us. She was not just my mother; she was my guiding star, my source of strength, and the embodiment of love. Her eyes sparkled with joy as she watched me take my vows.

In her loving and accepting nature, my mother welcomed my husband, who came from a different cultural background. She embraced not only him but also his family, reflecting her open-hearted spirit that transcended boundaries of race and ethnicity. It was a testament to her capacity for love and her ability to see the beauty in bringing people from different walks of life together.

As the celebration unfolded, my mother's presence became a beacon of happiness and warmth. She knew my friends, some of whom she hadn't seen in years, and her genuine interest in their lives made them feel truly valued. Family and friends alike gathered around her, sharing stories and laughter, creating a sense of togetherness that only she could inspire.

In the midst of revelry, my mother was a shining star, casting her radiant light over all of us. It was a day that she, too, cherished - a day where her love and happiness illuminated our hearts and made our wedding an unforgettable celebration of family and friends. This event remains etched in my memory as a profound symbol of her love and acceptance.

West Virginia/ Springfield, Virginia/Washington D.C.

(April 8, 1999-April 11, 1999)

On April 8, 1999, my mother embarked on yet another exciting journey, this time to the picturesque state of West Virginia. Accompanied by my sister, Thelma, they ventured to Charleston, where they were warmly welcomed by our cousin, Dr. Lagrimas Sadorra (Ging2), and her family. The initial two days were filled with heartfelt reunions and cherished moments.

But the adventure did not stop there. My mother, my sister Thelma, and Ging2, as the driver, set out on a memorable road trip to Virginia for a grand family event wedding of our cousin Vellie and her groom, Harry Hall.

The ceremony was held in Braddock, Virginia, and the celebration was held in the Hilton Hotel in Springfield, Virginia. This wedding was a true amalgamation of both sides of our family, with numerous relatives and friends coming together to celebrate.

As the festivities continued, my sister Mona Liza, my brother Emiliano, and I soon joined my mother in Virginia, bringing our own presence to the joyful occasion. A highlight of the trip was an exclusive river cruise along the Potomac River with family and friends. Onboard, the boat was adorned with delectable food, and the air was filled with the melodies of music and dancing. It was a splendid experience, and my mother reveled in every moment, cherishing the memories she was creating.

During her visit to Virginia, my mother had a remarkable opportunity that left her truly awe- inspired. Together with my aunt, they embarked on an unforgettable tour of the iconic White House in Washington, D.C. It was a momentous occasion as they strolled through the historic halls and rooms that have borne witness to chapters of American history. As they marveled at the grandeur and historical significance of the White House, my mother couldn't help but feel a deep sense of honor and pride. It was a glimpse into the heart of the nation, an experience she cherished as a true highlight of her journey.

New York Trip: Reconnecting With Friends from Hometown

(April 11-14, 1999)

After the joyous wedding celebration in Virginia, the adventure continued for my mother and her travel companions, my sisters Thelma and Mona Liza. They hopped on the train to the bustling metropolis of New York. The city that never sleeps welcomes them with open arms. Gina Alcordo was there to welcome them. As she wrote in her diary, they were entertained by Andrew Anderson. In day and Dick took them around the city of New York. They met with Senen Peque, and it was a reconnection of old friends and old town mates. She was amazed by their genuine hospitality.

In New York, they indulged in the rich history of the United States by visiting West Point, where future leaders of the nation were molded and explored the city of New York.

As they traversed the streets of New York, they dined in a multitude of restaurants, savoring the diverse sunshine the city had to offer. The shopping was another adventure, with boutiques and stores beckoning them to explore their treasures.

Their stay in New York was filled with hearty, warming reunions with old friends from our hometown. Laughter echoed through the streets as they reminisced about their shared pasts and created memories.

After a couple of days in the city that never sleeps, they embarked on their leg of the journey. With suitcases filled with cherished moments, they boarded a flight to sunny Florida, ready for more exciting adventures and her heartwarming reunions with family and friends. This time, her companion was my sister Thelma.

Florida Trip: Precious Time with Family

(April 14- 19, 1999)

Their final destination in this incredible journey was sunny Cape Coral, Florida, where the warmth of family greeted them with open arms. Eager in- laws, nieces, nephews, and their spouses embraced my mother and sister, Thelma, warmly, and the days ahead were filled with laughter and joy.

They were met at the airport by Tio Bobby and Tio Ramon with open hearts and joy. They stayed at Tio Bobby and Tia Panyang's place during their stay. As Sandy remembered, she visited my mother and Thelma at her parent's house during their stay, and together with my mother, they enjoyed baking her famous danish cookies, ensaymada and other delicious food.

At Tita's place, they indulge in succulent crabs and plump shrimps and the dining table became a place of hearty feasts and shared stories as they celebrated their time together. They spent quality time with Belen and Wilford, enjoying their outing at a well-known restaurant.

Bonds were strengthened, and memories etched into their hearts forever.

Gifts flowed in abundance, tokens of love and affection from relatives who were thrilled to have her among them. It was a time of togetherness and happiness that she cherished deeply.

As the trip neared its end, she reflected on the wonderful moments she had experienced throughout this incredible journey. Family, food, and festivities had been the cornerstones of this adventure, leaving her with a heart full of love and unforgettable memories. She ended her notes, "Our thanks to them. May our Lord Bless Them All. Goodbye Florida."

CHAPTER 28
RESILIENCE AND RECOVERY: OUR FAMILY'S MEDICAL JOURNEY

"The love of a family is life's greatest blessing" -by Eva Burrows

In the tapestry of life, moments of pure joy are woven alongside threads of resilience. In the midst of joyful travels and cherished moments, life sometimes takes an unexpected turn. Our narrative now shifts from the stories of adventures across oceans and continents to an event that would test our family's bonds like never before.

And while the memories of my mother's journeys to the US still sparkled in our hearts, a new challenge beckoned, one that would bring us closer together in a way we never imagined. In these pages, you'll find a story of love, determination, and the unwavering character of our family as we venture into the next chapters of this narrative, we step into a world where the colors are richer, the emotions deeper, and the challenges more profound. These are the stories of battles fought and hearts won, where our family's strength and love shone even brighter in the face of adversity.

Section 1: A Bond Of Life: Overcoming the Kidney Transplant Challenges

In March 1999, our family faced one of the most significant challenges in our history. It began with a letter from my brother Fred, which carried a plea for help. The news was devastating: he needed a kidney transplant to survive.

In the midst of our family's journey, when we faced the daunting prospects of my brother's need for a kidney transplant, our beloved mother became the beacon of strength. In the heartfelt letter, she gathered her thoughts, weaving a plea for help with threads of love and concern. Her words were not merely ink on paper; they were a testament to the unbreakable bonds of family. She called upon our shared faith, urging us to unite in prayer and to provide the financial support necessary for this life-altering endeavor. Knowing her children were scattered across the seas, she became the bridge that connected our hearts, reminding us that family is the cornerstone of our lives. Our mother's letter embodied her unwavering belief that together, we could overcome any challenge.

As we gathered to discuss his situation, the weight of the problem loomed large. We needed not only financial support but, even more critically, a suitable donor. Fred's wife, Amai, dedicated and loving as she was, couldn't provide a complete match. My brother, Alex, also stepped forward, eager to save his sibling, but medical tests revealed he wasn't the right candidate.

The desperate situation forced us to turn to the most unexpected source of help- our youngest sister, Judith. A devoted mother with her own family, she made a selfless choice to undergo the necessary tests, and to our astonishment, she was a complete match.

In the most challenging of times, my sister Judith emerged as a beacon of selflessness. Despite the anxiety and the responsibilities of her own family, she willingly stepped forward as the donor of our brother's kidney transplant. The knowledge I had gained, a nurse's insight, was my contribution to alleviating my sister's anxiety as the chosen donor. Her remarkable act of giving, of offering the gift of life, was a testament to the depth of familial love. Our hearts are forever filled with gratitude for the incredible sacrifice and the renewed life it brought to our family.

The medical evaluations and tests were conducted in Manila, and through this process, we were not just saving a life; we were cementing the bonds of our family.

The kidney transplant was performed, and miraculously, it succeeded. The victory was not only in saving Fred's life but in demonstrating the incredible strength and unity of our family.

However, the challenge was far from over. The financial burden that accompanied Fred's ongoing medical care and medication was immense. It took a village to shoulder the weight, and every member of our family contributed in whatever way they could. We pulled together not just to alleviate the financial strain but to provide emotional support, prayers, and boundless love.

For almost 17 years, Fred continued to live and thrive, a testament to the power of family bonds and extermination. The challenging chapter in our lives was marked by resilience, selfishness, and collecting effort. It is a story of strength, unity, and, most importantly, the unwavering love that binds our family together.

Section 2: Memoirs of Resilience: Navigating My Mother's Health Challenge

"A woman is like a tea bag- you can tell how strong she is until you put her in hot water."

In the chronicles of my mother's life, there is a unique chapter dedicated to her resilience in the face of health challenges. Through her meticulous documentation, she transformed her experience into a narrative of strength and courage. The chapter delves into her journey through a series of surgeries and an unexpected accident, demonstrating her unwavering spirit.

A. Hernia Operation (1986)

In 1986, my mother underwent a hernia operation and a partial colectomy. This was a moment that tested her physical strength and determination. Her meticulous notes from this period capture the blend of anxiety and hope that accompanied her to the hospital, despite the challenges, she emerged from this surgery with an indomitable spirit.

B. Cataract Operations (1998)

As the years advanced, my mother's vision started to wane due to cataracts. In 1998, she faced the issue head-on with two successive cataract surgeries, one for each eye. Her journal entries reveal her anticipation, as well as the joy of seeing the world with renewed clarity after the successful procedures.

C. Accident (2001)

Life can be unpredictable and in 2001. My mother encountered an unexpected obstacle in the form of a bus accident while walking. Hospitalized during this period, her words in her diary reflect her resilience and determination to recover. Her account of this incident serves as a testament to her unwavering spirit.

In the hospital, our family rallied around our mother. The accident had left her injured, but her spirit remained unbroken. Even as she lay in the hospital bed, she still wanted to be in control, offering instructions and guidance to her caregivers and family members who took turns attending to her. It was a testament to her unwavering strength and determination. In her own way, she was reassuring us that she was going to pull through, just as she always had during life's challenges.

My mother's documentation of her health issues and surgeries is a powerful narrative of courage and fortitude. Through the highs and lows of medical procedures and unexpected accidents, she demonstrated a remarkable ability to face adversity with grace. In my mother's meticulous journaling of her life, she took special care to document not only the events that brought her joy but also the challenges. This includes her encounters with the medical world, from surgeons who performed her surgeries, and her determination to record every detail extended to the costs she incurred, reflecting both her pragmatism and her dedication to keeping a comprehensive account of her life's journey.

These memories stand as a testament to her indomitable spirit and determination to embrace life's challenges.

Section 3: Resilience: A Journey from Fainting to Total Hip Surgery

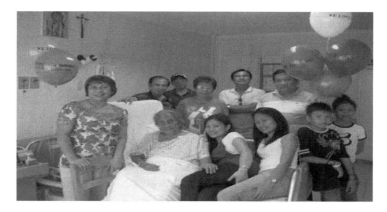

In the tapestry of my mother's life, there exists a vivid thread, a chapter etched with her unwavering intelligence and unwavering spirit. This tale recounts an extraordinary episode in her life when a sudden mishap revealed not only her fortitude but her sharp medical acumen. It was a journey that began with a broken hip but evolved into something profoundly meaningful.

The Faint and the Broken Hip

It all started with a fainting episode. One day, as my mother was opening the refrigerator, her world took a sudden, dizzying turn. She crumpled to the floor, and amidst the confusion and pain, her hip was broken. It was a shocking and painful experience, but it marked the beginning of her remarkable journey.

The Orthopedic Surgeon's Diagnosis

At the Hospital, an orthopedic surgeon, reviewing the X-rays of her broken hip, promptly informed her about the impending surgery. However, in the face of adversity, my mother's innate wisdom and instinct kicked in. She turned to the surgeon and said, "Not yet, until you find out why I passed out."

The Demand for a Cardiologist

With unyielding determination, my mother demanded the presence of a cardiologist. She recognized that there was more to her condition than a broken hip, and she insisted on a thorough investigation. The cardiologist's examination unearthed a starting truth- her heartbeat would intermittently stop.

The Pacemaker

In a fateful twist of her journey, a pacemaker became the first step. During her medical journey, my mother faced an unexpected hurdle. The doctors recommended a peacemaker for her heart, a device that would provide the steady rhythm her heart needed. But here's where it got complicated. In our small city of Cebu, obtaining such a sophisticated medical device during those days wasn't as straightforward as in larger metropolises. The process could take more than 24 hours. This presented a worrying question for my mother.

"What if my heart stops while I'm asleep?" she asked, her concern vivid on her face. The idea of waiting for the pacemaker, even for a day, seemed unbearable to her. She was, after all, a woman of action, unyielding in her desire to live a full and vibrant life.

In the face of this uncertainty, the medical team reassured her. They connected her to a holter monitor that remotely transmitted her heart's rhythm to the nurses' station, keeping a vigilant watch even as she slept. But it was this fervent determination, this fierce will to live, that set my mother apart. Her tenacity was a testament to the enduring strength of her spirit.

The pacemaker was implanted to regulate her heart's rhythm, ensuring its consistent, steady beat. My mother had not only questioned her diagnosis but sought the right answers. It was her resilience, intelligence, and assertiveness that led to this discovery.

The Total Hip Surgery

Only after the pacemaker was successfully implanted and her heart rhythms stabilized did she proceed with the Total Hip Surgery. Her recovery ordeal was remarkable, reflecting her unyielding spirit and the power of her quick thinking.

During her stay in the hospital for hip surgery, my mother's resilience and nurturing spirit shone through, even in the face of pain and vulnerability. She had always been a woman of great compassion, and she expected the same level of care she would have given to others.

I remember one incident vividly; it was when the nurses were helping reposition her. She felt their touch was less gentle than she would have liked, especially when she was in pain. In her determined and motherly way, she addressed the situation. She reminded them that she had children who were nurses, and they treated their patients with the utmost care and gentleness.

In her hospital room, she gave them a heartfelt lecture on how to handle patients with tenderness, drawing from her vast reservoir of maternal love. It was a testament to her unwavering commitment to kindness and compassion, even in moments of personal hardship.

This episode in my mother's life is a testament to her intelligence, strength, and her ability to advocate for her own health. Beyond the broken hip and the surgery that ensured it, it is a tale of resilience, determination, and the invaluable lesson that one should never hesitate to question one's diagnosis and seek the best possible care.

In the face of adversity, my mother showed remarkable resilience. She tackled her health challenges with unwavering determination, proving that age is just a number when it comes to fighting for one's well-being. Her medical journey is a testament to the strength of the human spirit and the power of mother's love.

CHAPTER 29
LASTING MEMORIES: MAMA'S FINAL VISIT TO THE US

(September 17 - December 31, 2005)

"Time together as a family is a gift" -by Joanna Gaines

In the twilight of her globe-trotting adventures, my mother embarked on her final journey to the United States. With my sisters, Evangeline and husband Bonnie, Judith, and Brother Leo and wife, they set foot once again on the land she'd come to know so well. My mother and my siblings stayed with me in Pleasanton, California. However, this trip was unlike any other. It was a grand occasion-wedding.

Sister's Wedding at Garre Winery, Livermore

On a bright sunny day at the enchanting Garre Winery, the event was set for a truly spectacular wedding of my sister Mona Liza to her groom, Steve Lowe. The winery's Martinelli Event Center, nestled amidst the rolling vineyards, provided a breathtaking backdrop that added a touch of magic to the occasion.

In the glow of that memorable day, as the golden sun kissed the horizon, my mother radiated a timeless elegance that took everyone's breath away. Her attire was the embodiment of grace and sophistication. Draped in a resplendent, flowing gown that simmered like moonlight on the water, she was the very image of ageless beauty.

Her smile was a testament to the happiness that swelled within her. It was a smile that bore the weight of wisdom and the richness of a life well-lived. Her eyes, aglow with happiness, spoke of many years she had spent nurturing and guiding her children.

The wedding was more than a family gathering; it was a reunion. Alongside the bride and groom, there were the faces of relatives and old friends, some from the other side of the globe she hadn't seen in years. Her eyes sparkled as she greeted them. Stories of bygone days flowed freely, reigniting connections that time has not diminished.

Despite her age, she danced with grace and ease. She proved that age is no barrier to joy, love, and celebration.

That day, at 87 years old, my mother looked and felt as radiant as ever. She was the living embodiment of the enduring love, happiness, and elegance that are the hallmarks of her remarkable life. Her presence was not just a blessing to the wedding but a vivid reminder that moments of happiness and elegance are ageless.

Sister's wedding pictures Sept. 23, 2005

The Grand Canyon Experience

As the sun rose over the vast expense of the Arizona desert, our family embarked on an epic road trip from Las Vegas to the Iconic Grand Canyon with Hillis and my niece Hazel. The journey itself was a remarkable experience for my mother, my sister Evangeline and her husband, Bonnie, and my brother Leo and his wife Minda.

The anticipation built as we approached the Grand Canyon, and when we finally arrived, we were greeted by an otherworldly sight. The sheer scale and grandeur of the canyon left us all, especially my mother, in a state of silent admiration. We explored the rim of the canyon, taking in its ever-changing hues and stunning vistas. At sunset, we gathered near the edge to witness the breathtaking transformation of the golden light painted on the canyon walls. It was a magical moment, a moment when my mother felt a connection to the natural world. It was a memory etched in our hearts, a testament to the beauty and wonder that the world has to offer. My mother was in awe and said, "Oh! God's Wonders"'

As we left the Grand Canyon after an overnight stay in one of the hotels and headed back to Vegas, we couldn't help but feel grateful for the time spent together as a family and for the opportunity to witness the majesty of the natural world.

Dazzled by Vegas: A Spectacular Showtime

Las Vegas, the city of lights and entertainment, held a special place in Mama's heart. One evening, we took her to see the iconic show "Mama Mia," a delightful spectacle of music, dance, and pure joy. Her eyes sparkled with excitement, and her heart danced to the rhythm of the music. As the performers brought the timeless melodies to life, she couldn't help but tap her feet and sing along. It was a magical experience that left her utterly engrossed on the show, a testament to her enduring love for music.

Another highlight of her time in Vegas was visiting the famous casinos. Slot machines, with their bright lights and jingling sounds, fascinated her. Sitting in front of one, she'd drop in a coin, pull the lever, and her face would light up with every spin. The thrill of winning, no matter the amount, made her feel like a child again. It was in these moments, amid the glitz and glimmer of the casino, that she found a simple but profound joy-that kind that brings a radiant smile to one's face, just like it did to Mama's.

Christmas Joy and Memorable Family Reunion (Christmas 2005)

In the warm embrace of our cozy family home in Las Vegas, the air was filled with laughter and love during our unforgettable Christmas reunion. It was a gathering like no other, an occasion that held a special place in our hearts. What made it so extraordinary? It was the presence of all six sisters, each coming from different corners of the world, to share this precious moment.

Jerry and Judith journeyed from the lively streets of LA, bringing with them the bright and sunny vibes of California. Mona and Steve made the trek from Tracy, California, a place where families love chores through the hills. Thelma, with her nieces and nephews, traveled from Pleasanton, California, her laughter and joy shining like a star.

Meanwhile, Leo and Minda, along with Eyen and Bonnie, made a long journey from the Philippines to join us in the heart of the United States. Their presence was a testament to the deep roots that connect our family, transcending borders and distances.

Our beloved mother, who was visiting the US during this memorable time, radiated happiness as she looked around at her six daughters together under one roof. It was a moment of unity, a testament to the powerful bond that family shares, no matter where life's journeys take them.

Christmas Eve had arrived, and the Sandalo-Golden household was a whirlwind of activity. The aroma of delicious dishes wafted through the air as the family busily wrapped presents, adorned the house with festive decorations, and prepared to celebrate the most cherished of holidays.

Unbeknownst to the rest of the family, Mama had her own preparations underway. She watched with a loving smile as her children, their spouses, and her grandchildren got caught up in the holiday spirit. Her gentle guidance and wisdom had always been the cornerstone of these joyous occasions.

As the evening approached, the family gathered around the table to enjoy a sumptuous Christmas feast. The laughter and camaraderie filled the room, and anticipation grew for the 'My Manito" tradition. In this heartwarming custom, each family member carefully selected a special gift for their secret recipient, accompanied by playful riddles and descriptions that made a guessing game a highlight of the night.

After the last present had been opened and much laughter had echoed throughout the house, Mama, with her usual grace, announced that she had something to share. Her children and grandchildren turned their attention to her as she was sitting in the middle of our gathering, with lights and a Christmas tree beside her, a serene smile on her face.

With the love and warmth that only a mother and a grandmother could exude, Mama delivered a heartfelt speech. Her words were a testament to the enduring bond of family, the power of love, and the significance of coming together during the holiday season. Her eyes sparkled with a mixture of joy and nostalgia as she spoke.

Our Christmas celebration was truly memorable, and here's Mama Moning's speech presented exactly as she said it.

"Beloved daughters, granddaughters, grandsons, sons-in-law and daughter-in-law: Holiday Greetings to you"

This evening, I share the pride and joy of our Family Reunion (just a small portion of our big family) on this Christmas Season, which provided the best occasion for other members of our family to come together and reaffirm their unity and affection with one another.

We are lucky indeed that we- Eyen, Judith, May, and I are here to attend the yearly Christmas celebration held in Becky and Hillis' beautiful home by which they are the hosts. We can also call this occasion a Christmas Family Reunion. This gathering is an expression of affection and unity with one another. With my greetings, I wish the spirit of brotherhood is manifested strongly by the members of our families in all the years to come and will stay forever. I congratulate this whole group for their oneness and concerns.

Let us strengthen the bonds (between us) not only by knowing our love and concern but by supporting one another. By doing so, we are supporting our relatives, brothers, and sisters and uplifting them and, at the same time, making our families the strongest and closest possible.

Tonight, as we gather for our Christmas Family Reunion, we are about to embark on a beautiful tradition of giving and receiving gifts. But, my dear family, let's not dwell on the material value of these gifts. Instead, let's measure them by the depth of love and care they carry.

Let's make this Christmas more than just a holiday season; let's make it a way of life. For instance, I recall a time when my eldest daughter, Thelma, needed a ride. At that moment, Jerome answered her call not just with a car but with his heart full of love. It's these everyday acts of love that truly make Christmas a part of our lives.

At this very moment, I feel happy watching you talk to one another, eat together, dance gracefully, smile, and even frown.

All that you do tonight to celebrate Christmas in a jolly, happy way- will be my sweet memories when I go home, and I will feel homesick. I'm too old to come back and join your fun as what you are doing tonight.

Lastly, I join you in thanking God for the success of our Christmas celebration. My warmest Greetings, Merry Christmas, and a Happy and Prosperous New Year. God Bless Us all."

Mama's Christmas speech became a cherished tradition in its own right. It was a moment that reminded everyone in the room of the deep love that bound us together as a family. It was a moment that captured the essence of what Christmas meant to the Sandalo Family: a time for love, joy, and togetherness.

In the glow of holiday lights and the warmth of familial togetherness, this Christmas reunion became etched in our memories as a testament to the power of love and unity.

Christmas Family Reunion 2005

CHAPTER 30
A HEARTFELT REUNION: STRONGLY UNITED IN 2007

"Our family is a circle of Strength; founded on faith, joined in love, kept by God, together forever"-Unknown.

In the years following my mother's last visit to the United States in 2005, our family embarked on a series of heartwarming reunions and joyous celebrations. These gatherings were not just a testament to the bonds that tie us together but a continuation of the legacy of love that our mother instilled in each of her children. Despite the physical distance that separated us, the spirit of unity and the memory of our beloved mother brought us together time and time again.

Over the years, several important dates were marked on our family calendar, assembled from various corners of the globe to honor our mother. In doing so, honor the values she cherished. A memory of a remarkable woman who will forever be the center of our attention.

Reuniting, Reconnecting, and Relaxing: The 2007 EMMO Sandalo Family Reunion

After our grand reunion in 1995, a remarkable twelve years passed, and we could gather once again for another grand reunion. This time, all the activities were held in Moalboal, our hometown.

In the heart of 2007, we embarked on a remarkable journey, a family endeavor that transcended borders, generations, and time itself. Our matriarch, the formidable and age-defying Mama at 89, stood as a testament to the enduring power of love and the importance of family. The seeds of this grand event were planted almost two years prior, as the idea of uniting our far-flung family began to take root.

Within the Sandalo clan, separated by oceans and continents, the notion of a reunion had been nurtured through the decades. The concept of renewing ties, rekindling memories, and creating new ones had always been present, simmering beneath the surface. It wasn't until one fateful conversation between families in the Philippines and sisters in the United States that the idea began to take form.

Amidst the technological limitations of the time, we painstakingly organized the reunion primarily through traditional means. It was a relentless pursuit with countless hours spent on the telephone and coordination of family members scattered across the globe.

The enthusiasm for the event was contagious. As children, grandchildren, nieces, nephews, and great-grandchildren were gradually pulled into the orbit of this extraordinary reunion, anticipation grew. It became a collective effort, with each family member contributing their ideas, talents, and resources. This event wasn't merely a family gathering; it was a living embodiment of the ties that had held us together for generations.

The forthcoming chapter delves into the intricate planning and the emotional build-up to the 2007 EMMO Sandalo Family Reunion, a monumental event that stands as a testament to the indomitable spirit of our family. In the following pages, you will experience the joyous and, at times labor-intensive journey of uniting our far-reaching family. The reunion was about much more than shared DNA; it was about rediscovering the threads that had woven our family tapestry over the years.

The story of our 2007 family reunion is an ode to love, unity, and unwavering determination. It's a testament to the incredible journey we embarked upon to celebrate the life and health of Mama, our beloved matriarch, and to strengthen the bonds that have held us together through the years.

Theme: Reunite, Reconnect, Relax

In 2007, our family reunion took on a special significance. It has been 12 years since our last grand gathering, and during that time, life has woven a rich tapestry for each of us. Our children had grown into accomplished professionals- doctors, nurses, engineers, and family members from all walks of life. Some had embarked on the journey of marriage and parenthood. My mother, the guiding force behind the reunion, sought to reunite us and reintroduce family members, both old and new generations, in an atmosphere of connection and discovery. Hence, our theme for this reunion is "Reunite, Reconnect and Relax" and have fun together once again.

Family Tree Color Theme/Logo Contest

As we were planning the reunion, we envisioned a meaningful way to identify each family, and this was through colors, each representing a branch of our family tree. Each color was chosen to honor a favorite of one of my siblings, making it uniquely special for each family. It was a visual mirroring the diversity and unity of our family, a beautiful testament to the love that bound us together.

Months before the grand reunion in 2007, the creative energy within our family surged with excitement as we announced the logo contest. This contest was an open call for my family members with an artistic flair to craft a design that encapsulated the essence of our reunion. We yearned for a symbol that would mirror the unity, warmth, and love that our family cherished.

The rules were simple: -create a unique logo that embossed the spirit of our reunion. It could be a hand-drawn masterpiece or a digital creation; the choice was entirely up to the artists within our clan. But what made this contest truly special was that it was not merely a competition; it was a celebration of our artistic diversity and shared creativity.

As the submissions flowed in, our family members were given the opportunity to cast their votes for the design that resonated with them the most. It was a fair and democratic process, with everyone having their say. The artwork had to speak to our hearts, reflect the essence of our family, and beckon to the nostalgia of our roots.

And then, the winner emerged. A design featuring two hands lovingly cradling a heart, all set against the backdrop of tropical trees. It was a symbol of our unity and the nurturing love that binds our family together. The chosen logo was a testament to our shared heritage, the caring hands of our ancestors, and the sheltering canopy of our family tree.

This contest was more than just a creative endeavor. It was a profound representation of our family's spirit. It encapsulated love, creativity, and unity that were the cornerstone of our reunion.

The Grand Reunion Begins- December 29,2007

Day 1: Arrival of Family and Bonding

The day had finally arrived, a day eagerly awaited by our family for over a decade. It was December 29, 2007, and the air was filled with a sense of anticipation and excitement as family members from various corners of the Philippines and "Balikbayan", those who had ventured far as American citizens but were returning to their roots, gathered for the grand reunion. The essence of togetherness was palpable, and the warmth of familial bonds was undeniable.

The day started with the distribution of reunion T-Shirts by Judith, each family choosing a color to represent them, a symbol of the intricate tapestry that makes up our family tree.

Then there was an afternoon with my mother, "Lola," as we affectionately called her, who was dedicated to the matriarch of our family with the grandchildren and great-grandchildren. This afternoon was coordinated by Hazel and Jessica, the oldest grandchild. Lola held court as the entire young generations of the family shared stories and caught up with one another.

As the sun began to set, we had a special dinner meeting for siblings only at Club Serena, at one of the beach houses in our town of Moalboal. This was a time for the core of our family to come together, reminisce and catch up with our life events and discuss the plans for the following days.

The first day concluded with lunch and dinner at Mama's house. Thelma, who stayed with Mama, ensured everything went off without a hitch. As we shared meals, we could already feel the magic of our family reunion beginning to weave its spell.

Little did we know that this was just the beginning of a three-day extravaganza that would not only unite us but also strengthen the bonds that held our family together. The memories we created during this reunion will be etched in our hearts forever.

Day 2: AM: Fun, Games and Family Bonding at EMGEN Park

The sun greeted us with its warm embrace on the second day of our reunion. It was a day filled with laughter, camaraderie, and endless fun. We had a special location in mind for this day-EMGEN Park, owned by my brother Emiliano and his wife Gehnee. This huge tennis court and park is in our hometown, Moalboal, just walking distance from our Mother's home.

The young and energetic members of our family, Jessie, Derrick, Farrah, Sabrina Sapphire, and Michelle, took the reins as leaders for the day. They organized an array of games and activities that brought out the child in all of us. It was heartwarming to see the different generations of our family coming together to participate, compete, and, most importantly, bond.

From morning until late afternoon, we engaged in friendly competitions, reliving our youth and creating memories that will be cherished for generations to come. It was a day filled with races, games, and team challenges. The sound of children's laughter echoed through the park, a testament to the joy that reverberated in our hearts.

We were 80 strong, with family members of all ages, from the youngest children to the wisest of seniors. To keep everyone energized and satisfied, we had a thoughtfully planned schedule for meals. It was divided into three sets of times to cater to children, juniors, and adults and seniors. This ensured that each family member enjoyed their meals in comfort.

As we came together for lunch and dinner, the essence of our reunion was perfectly encapsulated. A sense of togetherness, where each family contributed, whether through financial support or by bringing their unique flavors to our shared meals. We were not just having a family reunion. We were creating a lasting legacy of unity and love.

In the midst of all the excitement and games, it was heartwarming to remember that our roots were firmly grounded in this small town in Moalboal, where our mother, Lola, and the younger ones, resided. This reunion was not just about fun and games; it was about treasuring our family bonds, appreciating our shared history and looking forward to the years to come.

Day 2 was a beautiful chapter in the story of our family, a testament to the enduring love, laughter, and kinship. We eagerly look forward to the event in the evening of this wonderful day, knowing our time was indeed a precious gift.

Day 2: A Night to Remember: Grand Reunion's Dazzling Evening

On the evening of Day 2, our grand family reunion reached its pinnacle in the magnificent setting of the Activity Center, graciously hosted by my brother-in-law, Bonifacio Villanueva, who also happened to be the school president. The venue was perfect for our grand gathering, featuring a grand stand that would soon host an array of performances and a spacious covered area with elegantly set tables adorned with vibrant-colored shirts bearing our family logo.

Part I

Our program for the evening was thoughtfully planned and executed to perfection. Part 1 of the night was marked by a sumptuous dinner served to all attendees. We savored the delightful flavors of catered and served dishes, sharing stories and laughter while enjoying the camaraderie that only a family reunion can bring.

Part II

Part II was when the real magic happened. The program started with a touching prayer led by Sabrina, setting a reverent and united tone for the evening. A group of our youngest members took to the stage, singing a harmonious welcome song, which brought smiles to all of those present. Farrah, one of the more mature grandchildren, shared an inspiring message that resonated with our hearts, reminding us of the true significance of family.

My nephew Jessie, the loved and respected first doctor of the Sandalo family, gave the opening remarks, welcoming each one of us in a way only a family member could. He was eloquent, personable, and filled with warmth that defined our family.

As the night progressed, we witnessed a grand entrance. It was a breathtaking moment, with grandchildren and great-grandchildren parading onto the stage, showcasing the unity of our multi-generational family. The final act of Part II included two emotionally charged songs: "Celebration: and: If We Hold On Together." Which touched the hearts of all in attendance?

In Part II of the program, we transitioned into another segment that was equally as heartwarming.

Part III: A Symphony of Talent and Heartfelt Unity

Part III of our grand reunion unfolded like a symphony. Where love, talent, gratitude, and unity harmoniously blended into an unforgettable evening.

As the stage came to life, a kaleidoscope of talents painted a vibrant picture of the younger generation's abilities. Grandchildren and great-grandchildren, representing their respective family branches, took the spotlight. Each act was a brushstroke, painting a picture of our shared history. They conveyed stories through song and dance, reminding us of their resilience and creativity.

The grand stage was set, anticipation hung in the air like a sweet melody, and the family's hearts were filled with joy as we gathered around to witness something truly special. It was a culmination of days of practice and preparation. Each of us, the 12 children of Mama, had paired up 6 boys and 6 girls, ready to perform a beautifully choreographed dance.

Our youngest sibling, who was a talented dance instructor and choreographer, had crafted a routine. As the music began to play, we stepped onto the stage, representing our unity, love, and connection in a graceful way.

The audience, filled with family members of all ages, watched with awe and delight as we danced gracefully. Mama sat front and center, her eyes shining with pride and joy. She cheered us on, her heart overflowing with happiness, knowing that her children had come together to create something so beautiful.

The dance was a testament to the power of family, a symbol of the unity that had defined us over the years. It was a moment of pure celebration, a reflection of the love that had always connected us, and filled the room with an incredible warmth that would be cherished in our hearts forever.

But amidst this breathtaking display of youth and the special dance of the 12 children, it was the gesture of a quiet hero that stole the limelight. We paid tribute to our youngest sister, the true embodiment of selflessness. With unwavering courage and love, Judith donated her kidney to our ailing brother Fred. Our mother, the family's guiding star, took the stage and, with her heartfelt speech, honored her daughter's unparalleled acts of love. The emotions in the room were palpable.

Then, our brother, the beneficiary of this life-altering gift, found his voice. It quivered with profound emotion as he expressed the depth of his gratitude. With a lump in his throat, he acknowledged that had it not been for Judith's act of kindness, he wouldn't have been present at this heartwarming reunion. With our mother standing in between, they shared an intimate moment, a tableau of love, gratitude, and the indomitable bonds that define our family.

Amid the teary eyes and warm embraces, we celebrated the day's champions, awarding them for their spirit, dedication, and achievements in the morning's games.

The final speeches of the evening were delivered by my sister Eyen and myself. We extended our deepest appreciation to all who made this grand reunion a success. We acknowledged the significance of unity and the shared memories that would forever link us.

Then, it was my brother-in-law, Bonifacio Villanueva, who had the privilege of raising the final toast. A joyous cheer filled the room as we celebrated the love, the bonds, and the cherished memories that make us more than just a family. We are a formidable, loving unit.

But the moment that transcended all others was when we were asked by the master of ceremonies to raise our hands intertwined and to sing our Family song, "The Greatest Love of All." It was an ethereal moment. Tears of joy flowed freely, and the room reverberated with a chorus of love and unity. In that extraordinary instant, we were not just family; we were an embodiment of love, a testament to the power of unity.

Day 3: Celebrating Unity and Traditions/New Year's Eve

The evening of New Year's Eve was a highlight of our reunion. We engaged in a unique radiation- "party hopping'-moving from one home to another, whose homes are just steps away, to celebrate the New Year in the company of different branches of our family. The first stop was the Bucad's, followed by a joyful gathering at the Villanueva's, then to the Dionaldo's. Each of our sister's household had its unique flavor of festivities, but the common thread was the sense of togetherness that we cherished. Finally, we returned to Mama's house for the grand finale.

The night culminated in a spectacular fireworks display courtesy of the Villanueva's. The colorful bursts in the sky were symbolic of our close-knit family, a dazzling tapestry of love and unity.

Day 4: New Year's Day Activities

After an eventful and fun-filled New Year's Day Eve celebration, we began the New Year with a special program that ensured everyone had something to look forward to. The final day of our grand reunion was one that blended spirituality, tradition, and pure fun in the most heartwarming way. The mornings started with a Thanksgiving Mass, a tradition that allowed us to begin the year with a sense of gratitude and unity and a beautiful moment of reflection. My late brother, Alex, led and coordinated the service, guiding us in a shared moment of faith.

After the Mass, we paid a visit to the cemetery, a poignant but necessary part of our journey. It was my sister Jerry who took charge, guiding us through this solemn yet important ritual. We paid our respects to those who had passed but who were never far from our hearts. It was a moment to reflect on our roots and connect the past with our vibrant present.

As the day progressed, with spirits both lifted and grounded, we transitioned to an afternoon filled with sports and friendly competition at the EMGEN PARK. Each sport was meticulously managed. Emiliano directed the basketball tournament, while the late Fred supervised the badminton games. My sister Thelma, with her innate love for tennis, managed the tennis tournament. These games not only highlighted our competitive spirits but also our ability to unite under the banner of fun. It was a reminder that the family bonds grow stronger when we play together.

Continuing the Celebration

Our family never stopped celebrating. On New Year's day afternoon, the younger generation had their special time with Auntie Mona. While the grandkids and great-grandkids enjoyed delicious treats, my sister Mona shared stories of our family history and opportunities for taking pictures to keep track of our family tree.

For another delightful surprise, my daughter Karla and her husband Joseph hosted a beach party for the cousins on one of our beautiful beaches in our hometown, Moalboal. The day was filled with laughter, good food, and the soothing sounds of the waves. Our family always finds reasons to gather and make new memories.

Cousin's Night

The festivities continued with "Cousin's Night." In the heart of Cebu City, all cousins from various parts of the world came together. The event was generously sponsored by the "Balikpapan Cousins" -Hazel, Karla and Joe, Jerome and Liz, Sabrina, and Sapphire. It was an evening of delicious food, wine, shared laughter, and plenty of singing. Karaoke brought out the musical talents within our family, showcasing the vibrant connections across generations.

These activities added a layer of joy, connection, and tradition to our already memorable reunion.

In 2007, we celebrated not just the changing of the year but also the enduring love that bound us together. It was a memorable reunion, full of traditions, unity, and the unshakable affection we had for one another.

Lola Moning surrounded by her grandkids and greatgrandkids.

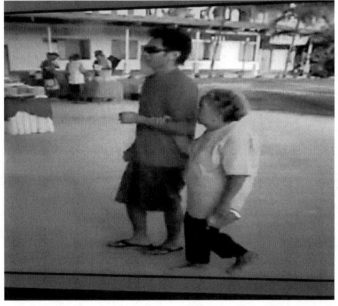

Reunion 2007

CHAPTER 31
GENERATIONS UNITE: THE 2010 FAMILY REUNION

"The Love in our Family Flows Strong and Deep, leaving us Memories to Treasure and Keep."

In the year 2010, a certain magic began to stir in the hearts of the grandchildren of Monica, our beloved mother. The family tree had grown, its branches stretching across the globe as children had grown into adults with professions, families, and lives of their own. It was time for the new generation to take the reins and create a reunion like no other.

The 12 siblings of Monica, who had been the stars of past gatherings, were now in the background, watching as their own offspring, a vibrant and diverse crew, took the lead. The gathering scheduled from December 28 to 31, 2010, stood out from previous ones. This time, the cousins took charge and orchestrated a delightful surprise for their parents, aunts, and uncles.

As the old year approached its conclusion, an extraordinary atmosphere enveloped everything. It was a reunion filled with anticipation, organized by the younger generation, and designed to create lasting memories for all. Let's embark on this unforgettable journey to discover how the grandchildren of Monica took the reins and crafted a reunion that would redefine family gatherings.

"A Grandkids' Grand Surprise"

In 2010, our family reunion took a new twist. This time, it was the grandkids who took the reins of planning and executing the event. What they had in store was beyond our wildest expectations.

Day 1

The excitement began on December 28th when the Balikbayans, those beloved members of our family returning from abroad, arrived. The first day was filled with laughter, chatter, and memories-what we call "Chika-Chika." It was a heartwarming start, with stories exchanged and bonds rekindled. It was also the meeting of the leaders of the event from abroad and the local chairman to finalize the details of the event. Yet, the true magic began on the 29th.

Day 2

A heartfelt Thanksgiving Mass united us, celebrating our family's enduring strength and unity. Afterward, we visited the cemetery to pay our respects to our ancestors, remembering their vital role in our family's story.

Lunch was back at Lola's house, filling the air with mouthwatering scents of traditional Filipino dishes. Mahjong tiles clinked, and the game's competitive spirit surfaced, echoing old traditions.

But the true climax awaited us that evening. The grandkids had orchestrated a white-themed bonfire dinner at EMGEN Park; the scene was nothing short of enchanting. Decorated with warm bonfires and adorned with white tents, the park seemed like a dreamland.

Everyone was in on the secret: wear white, they said. Then the time came when we were all informed that they were all ready for us to join them at EMGEN Park and, of course, a big pleasant surprise. As we approached the surprise bonfire, we were warmly welcomed by the grandkids, each of us draped with leis adorning our shoulders. The night was cloaked in darkness, illuminated only by the enchanting glow of the bonfire.

As my mother approached the entrance to the event, a radiant smile adorned her face. She was enveloped in an air of surprise and excitement. The pride in her eyes was unmistakable. This moment was the culmination of her dreams, a testament to the unity of her grandchildren, who had come together to craft a reunion beyond her wildest expectations. It was a scene etched into her heart, a moment of sheer joy and pride, eternally cherished in her memory. It was a clever twist, binding us all together in a sea of purity. The event started with a sumptuous catered dinner and was a feast for the senses.

Amidst the velvety darkness of that starry night, the 2010 family reunion was graced by the most enchanting event. It began with the youngest members of the family, each holding a candle, their innocent voices echoing the sacred words of "Our Father." A sea of flickering flames and torches set the scene for what was to follow.

As the bonfire crackled and danced, our stunning cousins took center stage, performing a mesmerizing belly dance beautifully choreographed by the talented Ebon. This was swiftly followed by the dynamite, high-energy hip-hop dance, an impressive display of rhythm and style meticulously taught by the talented duo Sapphire and Sabrina.

Then came the moment that unified us all dance, featuring every cousin moving to the beats of Shakira's "Waka-Waka." , The official 2010 FIFA World Cup song. It was a spirited spectacle that brought us closer, reinforcing the bond that ties us together through love of dance and music.

To top it off, the 8-year-old Nicole, Janice's daughter, graced the night with her melodious voice with the song "This Is Me" by Demi Lovato. Her soulful rendition left us all in awe and moved our hearts in ways that words can't describe. It was a magical night under the starlit sky, filled with family, fire, and a symphony of talents that resonated with our souls.

As the night of our extraordinary Bonfire event unfolded, there was an unexpected surprise that left a lasting impact on all of us. Karen Villanueva, my cousin's daughter, Mimi, from my father's side, who was known as the City Mayor at Bais City, Negros Oriental, arrived at the gathering, and her presence alone was heartwarming. Karen had a spontaneous yet profoundly inspiring speech that she shared with all of us.

With wisdom and grace, Karen quoted Khalil Gibran's powerful words: 'You are the bows from which your children, as living arrows, are sent forth.' Her words resonated deeply with all of us, reminding us of the importance of family, unity, and the enduring legacy we carry forward from our ancestors. Karen's surprise appearance and her touching speech were among the highlights of that unforgettable night, reminding us of the profound connection that binds our family together.

The night was a revelation symbol of the bonds that ran deep in our family and the continuity of love and traditions. And it was all thanks to the grandkids, whose dedication and creativity turned this family reunion into a magical experience we would never forget.

Day 3

The third day of the reunion began with a hearty breakfast at Lola's house, a perfect way to fuel up for the exciting day ahead. The main event of the day was the highly anticipated Sports fest, where family members of all ages engaged in various games and competitions held at EMGEN PARK. The spirit of friendly competition filled the air, creating a lively and energetic atmosphere.

After a fun-filled morning, everyone gathered at Lola's house for a delicious lunch. The hearty meal provided the perfect opportunity to rest and recharge before the afternoon activities.

Post-lunch, a short siesta allowed everyone to catch a breather and rejuvenate. Then, the activities resumed, with special games for the younger children and a range of fun activities to engage family members of all ages. Laughter and joy filled the air as generations came together to enjoy each other's company.

As the sun began to set, the day culminated in a delightful dinner once again at Lola's house. The evening festivities continued with a Karaoke session held at the Villanueva's residence, providing a stage for family members to showcase their musical talents or simply enjoy each other's performances.

The third day of the 2010 reunion was a testament to the enduring bond of family and the importance of coming together to create lasting memories.

Dedicated Organized Team:

The success of the 2010 family reunion was a testament to the incredible teamwork and dedication of our grandkids, who worked tirelessly to ensure every detail of the event was flawlessly executed. Each cousin, whether a Balikbayan or a local in the Philippines, played a vital role in this grand endeavor.

Hazel and Karla, who were overseas, took on the challenging task of chairing the event, showing their leadership despite the distance. Sheila, in the Philippines, provided valuable insights and coordination.

The Amusement Board, led by Doc. Jesse and Derrick ensured that our program was filled with joy and entertainment. Jerome and JP masterfully organized the sports events, while Janice, Farrah, Sabrina, Sapphire, Daffodil, and Quennie orchestrated delightful games that brought laughter to every corner of the reunion.

For accommodations, Alexis, Bryze, OJ, and Emem took charge, ensuring that everyone had a comfortable and convenient stay. A special mention to Steve, Jonathan, Tom, Ken, and Jason, who work diligently to set up and clean up the event space, allowing the festivities to run seamlessly.

Transportation logistics were managed by Steve and Tom, making sure everyone got to the right place at the right time. Their efforts behind the scenes were crucial to the smooth operation of the reunion.

The dedication and commitment of each grandkid were truly inspiring. It was their unity and coordinated effort that made the 2010 reunion a memorable and unforgettable experience for the entire family. We are immensely grateful for their hard work and passion.

CHAPTER 32
LOLA MONING: THE HEART OF OUR GRAND FAMILY

"A grandmother's love is forever and always"-Unknown.

In the warmth of her embrace, we found a haven of love and wisdom. This chapter is dedicated to a role that brought a new dimension to our beloved Mama, one that she cherished and embraced with all her heart: that of a grandmother, "Lola," as the grandchildren affectionately call her. Through the eyes and voices of her grandkids, as well as the words of cousins, friends, and relatives, we embark on a journey to explore the love, laughter, and lessons that radiated from her as our family's matriarch. Join us as we delve into the endearing tales of Mama's life as Grandma, where her legacy continued to flourish.

ANECDOTES FROM MY NEPHEWS

In the embrace of Lola's love, three young hearts found a treasure trove of wisdom, laughter, and life lessons. The bond between these nephews and their Lola was unique. Growing up, they had the privilege of living under the same roof as their beloved Lola, creating a special connection that only grew stronger with time. Mama used to teach them patiently in their studies during their elementary school days. As the years passed, their visits to Lola's home in Moalboal became cherished traditions, bringing them closer to the heart of the family.

In the following anecdotes, these nephews and nieces, each with their distinct perspectives, share the stories and moments that capture the essence of Lola's remarkable presence in their lives. Let's embark on a journey through their memories and experiences, where Lola's love and wisdom illuminated their paths.

ALEXEIS' ANECDOTES

(1)

Alexeis recalls a memorable incident that perfectly captures Lola's spirit of generosity and her love for the grandkids. It was during one of his visits to her house in Moalboal, during the semestral break, and the evening was unfolding just like any other. Alexeis and his cousin, Tom, were enjoying some hard rock music in Lola's cozy home. The clock struck 8 pm., and Lola, ever the perceptive and caring grandmother, noticed the young duo's presence.

She approached them, tapping her leg, and in her typical loving manner, asked, "Aren't you guys going out tonight?" To this, Alexeis and Tom responded with youthful honesty, "No, Lola, we don't have any plans to go out this evening." Still, they were content with their music and time together.

But Lola, with her heart brimming with affection, had other ideas. Suddenly, she stood up and told them to have fun, insisting,"

251

Here are 500 pesos." To the young hearts of Alexeis and Tom, that sum was a small fortune, a delightful surprise that made the evening even more special. In this simple yet profound gesture, Lola's love and care for her grandkids shone through, leaving an indelible mark on their memories and hearts.

(2)

During one of the most critical moments of our lives, Lola faced some health challenges. Alexeis recalled that he was faced with a unique and unforgettable situation. At that time, he was in preparation for the upcoming board exam. He found himself at a crossroads: "Who would look after Lola?"

"Without hesitation, I knew I had to step up. Lola had always been there for all of us, showering us with love and care. It was my turn to return that love."

On my birthday, the 9th of May, I had an unconventional celebration in mind. I decided to bring the festivities to Lola's hospital room. I went to a nearby fast-food restaurant and ordered a special meal- one piece of chicken and an order of spaghetti and a burger. It wasn't a lavish feast, but it was more than just food; it was a gesture of love and appreciation for my beloved Lola.

Lola's eyes lit up with a mixture of surprise and joy. We shared that simple yet profoundly meaningful meal together. It was a celebration of life, of our bond, and the love that transcended any challenge life threw our way. It was an experience that left an indelible mark on my heart, a testament to the strength of our family ties and the immeasurable importance of love between a grandmother and her grandchild."

(3)

"One vivid memory that I hold dear was the day I decided to introduce my girlfriend, Chelen (now my wife), to Lola. Living on my own at Auntie Joji's place, Lola often expressed her traditional values. She told me not to bring girls into her house. So, this felt like a significant step.

I decided to visit Lola with my girlfriend, and to my surprise, she didn't object. I remember telling her I wanted to cook chicken curry, and she even helped me clean the chicken herself. The simple act spoke volumes to me. It was a sign of acceptance and love, showing that, despite her traditional beliefs, she was open to welcoming new members into our family. It was a heartwarming experience that reinforced how special my Lola was in embracing change and welcoming my girlfriend into her home."

ANDRE'S MEMORABLE MOMENTS WITH LOLA

(1)

Every summer, young Andre would journey from bustling Manila to the serene town of Moalboal, where his beloved Lola Monica resided. The mere sight of her would lit up his world, and these visits became precious traditions. However, as every vacation neared its end, the heart-wrenching moment of departure arrived.

With a heavy heart, he would say, 'Lola, I'm going back to Manila." Monica, ever the caring matriarch, would silently retreat to her room. Moments later, she'd return, a warm smile on her face, handing Andre 200 pesos.

"Here is your fare for the bus.", she'd say. It was a small gesture that meant the world to him. A token of her love, a reminder of her kindness.

And it wasn't just the money. It was the knowledge that his Lola cherished him, missed him, and wished him well on his journey back to the city. Those simple yet profound moments etched Lola's love deep within his heart.

As he said, "Lola is always in my heart. She was so sweet, caring, and thoughtful."

In fact, Monica's love was so profound that it transcended generations. It was through her loving influence that Andre named his daughter after her, passing on her memory and gentle wisdom to the next of kin.

(2)

"During my college years, I was pursuing a degree in "Marine Engineering," and Lola, always with her sense of humor, never missed a chance to tease me. She'd ask with a twinkle in her eye, "Andre, where's your boat docked today?" In "Tulay?" (a little pier in Moalboal).

Now, as I travel around the world in my career, I can't help but miss those moments when I could share my adventures and experiences with Lola."

Lola's presence was an integral part of their lives, and how they miss those interactions.

ANDREW'S ANECDOTES WITH LOLA

(1)

One memorable incident that Andrew vividly recalls is when the three brothers, Alexeis, Andre, Andrew, and their late father, Alex, were celebrating one of their brother's birthdays in a quaint little place in Moalboal. They had gathered for a meal and some quality time together. However, their grandmother, Lola, unexpectedly made an entrance. It seems they had forgotten to extend an invitation to her. Her reaction was swift and unapologetic. Lola scolded them all, particularly their father, for not extending a proper invitation. The unexpected visit and her candid words left an indelible mark on their memory.

(2)

As children, my nephews, Alexeis, Andre, and Andrew, were avid fans of cartoons. They'd gather around the television and watch these colorful characters with wide, exaggerated eyes. But every time they tuned in, Lola, with a moisture of curiosity and bemusement, would pose the same question. "Why are you not afraid of cartoons?" They have such big eyes!" And we'd all share a hearty laugh, a simple yet enduring memory of our times with her.

ANECDOTES FROM DERRICK AND JAMES

DERRICK'S MEMORIES OF LOLA

(1)

In the 1990s, the cousins knew that there was an unwritten rule when visiting Lola's house. They knew that to watch TV or listen to music, permission was a must. But what stood out, particularly to my nephew, Derrick, was the sacred "refrigerator rule. You do not dare open it without Lola's consent".

It was an unspoken law etched into childhood memories. Yet what truly struck Derrick was the occasional bending of this rule. Lola, who could be stern in her ways, would sometimes allow us to flout this particular guideline. It was as if she held a secret spot for those who dared to disregard her fridge decree.

Derrick, like the rest of us, saw this as a testament to Lola's boundless love. Her strictness was a surface layer, but underneath, she was an embodiment of warmth and understanding. She would, at times, break her own rules to indulge their youthful desires, teaching us an invaluable lesson in the art of balance and compassion.

(2)

Derrick fondly remembers that every time he visited Moalboal, Lola would secretly inquire about his favorite foods. This thoughtful gesture revealed her caring nature as she would send someone to the market to buy those special treats for him.

(3)

Generous Lola: During one of her visits to the city, Lola noticed Derrick's collection of X-Men cards. Not only did she take an interest in his hobbies, but she also promised to share some of those collectibles with Andre and Andrew. This anecdote reflects her selfless, thoughtful, and generous spirit.

MEMORIES FROM JAMES (EM-EM)

After years of living in the same town as Lola, the occasion for a deep conversation finally arrived in the aftermath of Typhoon Yolanda. It was during this challenging time that Lola imparted to James, fondly known as Em-Em, some invaluable wisdom. She spoke of the qualities that make a good father, much like his own grandfather, and emphasized the importance of improving one's life.

Em-Em, inspired by her words, dedicated himself to both work and study. He worked on days for family, while nights were devoted to his education. Lola's encouragement provided the motivation he needed to strive for a better future.

During their heartfelt conversation, she also expressed her fondness for Em-em's daughter, Rain. In a playful tone, she remarked that she wished Rain had been named after her. It was during these moments that Lola's unique sense of humor and love shone brightly.

In the end, this memorable interaction earned Em-Em and family a special nickname from Lola- "the survivors," a testament to their resilience in the face of life's challenges.

ANECDOTE FROM THE YOUNG AND RESTLESS NIECES

Summer vacations in Moalboal were always a much-anticipated adventure for my young, spirited, and restless nieces Hazel, Ebon, Sheila, Farrah, Michelle, and Queenie. The highlight of their visits was undoubtedly the precious time spent with our mother, their Lola. They stay at their parents' houses, just a stone's throw away from Lola's humble abode.

However, Lola Moning had a rule that she held dear: no staying out late at night, a decree she enforced with unwavering diligence; her curfew was a strict 8 pm. And she took her role as the guardian of their bedtime seriously. Yet my nieces, full of youthful exuberance and mischief, often conspired to test her resolve.

With the moon casting a silvery glow on Moalboal's quiet streets, they would wait until the house seemed to have fallen into a deep slumber. Giggles would echo through the night as they hatched their escape plan, convinced that Lola was fast asleep.

Softly, they would slip out of the house, their hearts pounding with excitement.

Little did they know that Lola possessed a sixth sense, especially when it came to her granddaughters. As soon as she sensed their mischievous intentions, in the darkness, she flicked on a light, casting unexpected light on their clandestine adventure. Startled and caught red-handed, my nieces would be greeted by her knowing smile. Their attempts to outwit her became a nightly ritual. It was a game of cat and mouse, filled with laughter and the thrill of breaking the rules, but Lola always had the upper hand.

These clandestine escapades were a testament to the enduring bond between Lola Monica and her granddaughters. While they playfully tested her limits, they also cherished the love and protection she provided. Her watchful eye and the glow of that late-night light served as a reminder that, no matter how much they grew, they could always count on the unwavering care for Lola.

LOLA'S CLASSROOM: A HAVEN OF LEARNING AND LAUGHTER

In the days when the grandchildren graced Lola's home with their presence, a remarkable transformation would unfold. Lola's cozy living room, typically a haven of quietude, would morph into a lively classroom, pulsating with the contagious energy of excitement and curiosity."

For Lola, education is a celebration, and she marks their achievements with songs, turning lessons into joyful duets. Her special stash of chocolates and cookies is always ready to reward their efforts, sweetening their learning experience.

The older grandchildren and neighboring children, too, find themselves drawn into Lola's unique classroom. Those boasting perfect scores are playfully retested, their claims met with good-natured skepticism. They present their test papers, and Lola, ever the astute teacher, verifies their achievements. A correct answer earns them not just her approval but also a few coins, a tangible sign of her pride and joy in their success.

Lola's home is more than just a place; it's a space where education blends with love, where learning is filled with laughter, and where every visit leaves her grandchildren enriched and cherished.

In the tapestry of our family's story, the voices of Monica's grandchildren shine brightly. Their anecdotes paint a vivid picture of a Lola who embodied love, generosity, humor, and unwavering care. Her impact on their lives is immeasurable, and they carry her lessons of discipline and laughter with them always. As they reminisce about their cherished Lola, one thing is abundantly clear: her love lives on in their hearts, a timeless legacy that will continue to shape their lives for generations to come.

CHAPTER 33
GRAND CELEBRATION: MONICA'S 95TH BIRTHDAY REUNION 2013

"The Love of a Family is a Life's Greatest Blessing"

Ninety-five years—a remarkable journey filled with love, laughter, and countless cherished moments. As we gather the threads of my mother Monica's extraordinary life, there's one chapter that stands out as a testament to the enduring power of family bonds and the joy of celebrating a life well-lived. It was a grand two-day event, a reunion like no other, and a birthday celebration that would forever be etched in our hearts.

In this chapter, we step into the heartwarming embrace of a family scattered across the globe, siblings who traveled from distant corners of the world to converge on one unforgettable occasion. The occasion? The 95th birthday of our beloved matriarch, Monica, or "Lola," as she's affectionately known to her many grandchildren and great-grandchildren.

The air was filled with anticipation as siblings reconnected after years apart, bridging the miles with warm embraces and joyful laughter. It was a time of shared stories and loving reminiscences, where generations came together to honor the woman who had been the steadfast anchor of our family.

Over two remarkable days, we celebrated Monica's incredible journey, one that had seen her weather life's storms with grace and resilience. We reveled in the beauty of her wisdom and the enduring warmth of her love. This chapter unfolds the tale of a milestone marked not by age alone but by the enduring legacy of a mother, grandmother, and great-grandmother whose love has touched us all.

Join us as we relive the magic of Monica's 95th birthday celebration, where love knew no boundaries and where the bonds of family were celebrated grand style. It was a reunion that reminded us that, no matter where life takes us, our hearts will always find their way back home—to Monica, our guiding light and the source of our greatest joy.

THE FIRST DAY: ARRIVAL OF SIBLINGS AND FAMILY MEMBERS

The excitement was palpable as siblings and family members from far-flung corners of the world descended upon Moalboal, our beloved hometown. The air was filled with anticipation and the echoing laughter of cousins reuniting after years apart. It was a homecoming like no other, a testament to the enduring bonds of family.

For our traditional sibling meeting, we gathered at my brother Emiliano and Gehnee's house, nestled amidst the familiar sights and sounds of Moalboal. In the midst of our traditional delicious Filipino luncheon, we finalized plans for the grand celebration that lay ahead. The meeting was not merely a formality; it was a heartfelt catch-up session where stories of adventures, trials, and triumphs were shared.

THE SECOND DAY: "MANIANITA"- A MAGICAL SERENADE

Then came the crack of dawn on the second day, may 4th, a date etched in our hearts as the actual birthday of our beloved Monica. It was around 4 am, a time when the world was still wrapped in the embrace of night, that something truly magical unfolded.

A hushed excitement filled the air as the tradition of "Manianita" commenced. In the gentle darkness of the early morning, a group of serenaders gathered, carrying the gift of music and warmth. These were not just any singers; they were a diverse group that included our own grandkids, dear neighbors, old friends, and the young and old alike.

With candles in hand and bouquets of flowers, they serenaded the birthday celebrant with a melodic blend of birthday tunes and folk songs. The notes of their songs seemed to harmonize with the whispers of dawn, creating an atmosphere of pure enchantment.

As we helped our mother rise from her slumber and led her to the front door, she was greeted by a tableau of love and devotion. The soft glow of candles illuminated the faces of her loved ones, young and old, as they sang and swayed to the music. It was a moment that brought tears to our eyes, a moment where the passage of time seemed to stand still, and the beauty of family bonds was never more apparent.

In the quiet, early dawn of Moalboal, with the scent of flowers and the gentle flicker of candles, we celebrate not just a birthday but a life filled with love and enduring connections. The "Manianita" was not just a tradition; it was a testament to the love that surrounded our mother, and it marked the beginning of a day that would be cherished for generations to come.

CONTINUATION OF THE "MANIANITA;" BREAKFAST AND THANKSGIVING MASS

As the melodious strains of the Manianita serenade slowly faded into the morning air, a sense of unity and love enveloped us all. The serenaders, still holding their candles and flowers, were invited to join us for a heartfelt breakfast. This meal, generously sponsored by my sister Jerry and her family, was a warm and inviting gathering that reinforced the spirit of togetherness.

The breakfast table was adorned with a delightful array of traditional Filipino dishes, from the aroma of freshly brewed coffee to the sweet scent of pandesal, a beloved local bread, sweet rice cakes, and many more delicious breakfast dishes. It was a time for hearty laughter and shared stories, a precursor to the day's grand festivities.

After the satisfying breakfast, the day's schedule called for a Thanksgiving Mass at 930 am. It was a moment of solemn reflection and gratitude, where every family member, young and old, gathered to offer thanks for the blessings of love, life, and family. The church's pews were filled with our voices lifted in prayer and song, a harmonious chorus of thanks that resonated throughout the sacred space. Then, a traditional cemetery visits after church to pay respects to our ancestors.

Bonding Time with Lola: Lunch and Precious moments

Following the Thanksgiving Mass, the day unfolded with a beautiful simplicity that reflected the essence of family. At 1130 am, we all gathered at Lola Monica's house for an intimate bonding time. The atmosphere was filled with laughter and affection as we surrounded her, our beloved matriarch, with love.

Lunch was graciously provided by my sister Thelma, who had prepared a feast. Traditional Filipino dishes, each with a story and a memory of its own, adorned the table. As we savored the flavors of our hometown and shared tales of our childhood, it felt as if time had stood still.

The walls of Lola's home bore witness to decades of family gatherings and celebrations, and on this day, they echoed with the joy of generations coming together. Children played, adults reminisced, and Lola Monica, the radiant center of it all, soaked in the love that surrounded her.

It was a day that celebrated not only Monica's 95 years of life but also the boundless love that flowed through the veins of our family. It was a day of traditions, togetherness, and treasured moments, a testament to the enduring legacy of our remarkable mother and grandmother, and a reminder that, no matter where life takes us, the heart always finds its way back to the family.

A Night of Celebration: Monica's 95th Birthday Evening

As the sun began its descent on that unforgettable May 4th evening, the atmosphere was charged with excitement and anticipation. The stage for the grand celebration was set on the spacious balcony of my brother's house, overlooking the front yard adorned with tents and tables for the catered special dinner. It was a sight to behold, a beautiful fusion of festivity and togetherness.

Before indulging in the sumptuous meal, a moment of reflection and gratitude was shared. It was our Doc Jess, a beloved grandchild, who led the way with a heartfelt prayer for dinner. His words resonated through the evening air, a reminder that this celebration was not just about the festivities but also about the blessings of family and togetherness.

Following a delectable dinner, a hush of anticipation fell over the gathered family and friends as a magnificent multi-tiered birthday cake was wheeled out. This grand cake was presented with love from my sister Jerry and her family, a testament to their adoration for Monica. The room was filled with the sweet voices of Monica's grandkids, Leo and Minda's family, singing joyful birthday songs. The heartfelt melodies filled the air, carrying the collective wishes of love, happiness, and good health for the birthday celebrant.

The entertainment continued as grandchildren from different families took center stage, showcasing their talent and creativity through dance performances. Each presentation was a tribute to Monica's vibrant spirit and the love she had instilled in each of them.

The momentous occasion also saw heartfelt speeches from the siblings, each sharing their personal stories of growing up under Monica's guidance and the profound impact she had on their lives. Tears of nostalgia and gratitude mingled with laughter as they recalled cherished memories and lessons learned from their remarkable mother.

But perhaps the most touching moment of the evening was when Monica herself took center stage. With grace and a twinkle in her eye, she took the microphone and delivered a speech that touched every heart in the room. Her words were a tapestry of wisdom, love, and humor. She shared numerous anecdotes from her journey through life, regaling the audience with the stories that had us in stitches.

Yet beneath the humor, there was a profound wisdom that only comes with age and experience. My mother's speech was a testament to the resilience of the human spirit, the power of love, and the importance of cherishing every moment.

As the night wore on, the celebration transformed into a lively Karaoke session, with the younger generations taking the stage. The air was filled with melodies and laughter as the night turned into the early hours, a fitting culmination to a day filled with love, laughter, and cherished memories.

Monica's 95th birthday evening was not just a celebration of her remarkable age; it was a celebration of a life well-lived, a tribute to the enduring bonds of family, and a reminder that love and laughter are the greatest gifts we can give and receive.

THE THIRD DAY: LEGACY OF LOVE: "MAMA'S SURPRISE INHERITANCE"

In the annals of our family history, the year 2013 holds a special place year that witnessed a birthday and reunion like no other. Mama, at the sprightly age of 95, decided it was the perfect time to gather her beloved children once more. The occasion was a joyous celebration that spawned three unforgettable days filled with laughter, reminiscences, and family bonds.

266

On the third day of our jubilant festivities, we were summoned to gather around Mama's cozy living room. The anticipation hung in the air as we sat expectantly, wondering what Mama had in store for us. It was a moment we would soon come to cherish, a moment that encapsulated her unwavering love and foresight.

Mama emerged from her room, her eyes sparkling with a mixture of excitement and wisdom earned through the years. In her hands, she held a handful of folders, each bearing the names of one of her children, each containing documents and titles of land properties. It was a revelation that left us momentarily stunned, for we had no inkling of the treasure trove of inheritance she had prepared.

The significance of her actions became clear as she handed each of us a folder. These documents represented her land properties, which she had meticulously surveyed and equally divided into twelve portions when she was 77 years old. Back then, in 1995, she had prepared numbers corresponding to the land numbers on the map, and we had drawn lots during our grand reunion. Little did we realize that this gesture was a promise that came to fruition in 2013.

The room was filled with a mix of emotions, gratitude, and a touch of melancholy. It was a moment of pleasant surprise, one that was tinged with the bittersweet realization that this was a significant chapter in our family's journey. Amidst the laughter and hugging our mother, our late brother Fred couldn't help but quip, "Thank you. I felt like we were receiving our diplomas at graduation."

Mama's decision to officially distribute our legal inheritance from her was more than just a financial gesture. It was a poignant reminder of her love, her wisdom, and her desire to ensure our futures were secure. It was a testament to her enduring role as the matriarch of our family, a role that extended far beyond the boundaries of time.

In the tapestry of time, moments like Mama's 95th birthday reunion shine with a brilliance that leaves an indelible mark on our hearts. It was a day of joy, unity, and boundless love celebration that transcended age and circumstance.

As we reflect on that remarkable day, we are reminded that family is the true treasure in our lives. Mama's enduring love and the bonds that bind us are the greatest gifts we could ever receive.

In that precious moment when she handed us our inheritance, Mama bequeathed to us more than just land; she gave us a legacy of love and a reminder that family is the cornerstone of our existence.

With hearts full of gratitude and cherished memories, we move forward, carrying the warmth and love of that celebration with us. Mama's 95th birthday reunion was more than an event; it was a testament to the enduring power of family, a legacy that will forever light our path.

CHAPTER 34
LEGACY OF LOVE: MONICA'S 97TH BIRTHDAY REUNION 2015

"Legacy of Love: It is not what you leave for your loved ones, but what you leave in them" Unknown

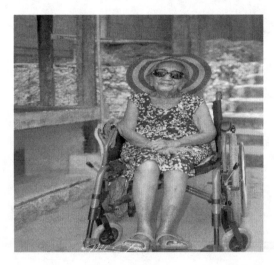

In the grand tapestry of our family's history, there was a moment that stands as a testament to love, unity, and the enduring bonds that span generations. The year 2015 marked the celebration of a remarkable life, a life that we cherished more deeply than we ever imagined, and it was a celebration that saw the Sandalo family come together in a way like never before.

This chapter unveils the story of a grand reunion that was unlike any other as we gathered to celebrate Monica's 97th birthday. It was a day filled with joy and festivities, a day where generations converged to honor the matriarch of our family. Little did we know that this joyous occasion would become our last family gathering with our beloved mother.

The preparation for this monumental day was nothing short of exhilarating. Organized by the grandchild generation, their energy and excitement infused the planning with a vibrant spirit. Simultaneously, the siblings, always the pillars of our family, were eager to ensure that the celebration would be as memorable as it was heartfelt.

But there was a twist in the tale, a delightful surprise that added an element of friendly competition to the preparations. While the siblings meticulously crafted their plans, the grandchild generation had a secret plan of their own, one that would soon be revealed with great fanfare.

As we delve into the details of the celebration, we marveled at the unity and love that fueled our family's preparations. What made this occasion even more extraordinary was the sheer number of attendees who came home from different places in the Philippines and abroad. The Sandalo family had grown in number, swelling to perhaps around a hundred or more, including in-laws. It was a testament to the strength of our familial bonds, a gathering that followed five previous grand-family reunions.

Join us as we journey through the excitement, the surprises, and the heartfelt moments of Monica's 97th birthday reunion. In the midst of laughter and joy, we celebrated a life well-lived and the love that would continue to unite us, even in her absence. It was a day that showcased the strength of our family's ties, a day that would forever hold a cherished place in our hearts.

MANIANITA: A DAWN SERENADE OF LOVE

In the calm quiet of the early morning on May 4th, a special thing happened—a beloved custom called Manianita, a sweet serenade that made Mama's 97th birthday really special. The clock read 4 a.m. and a group of young grandchildren and friends gathered, their voices a gentle chorus that carried through the quiet morning air. The enchanting melodies of "Happy Birthday" and cherished folk songs graced our ears. It was a serenade of a heartfelt expression of love and admiration for the woman who had touched our lives so profoundly.

With great care and anticipation, we helped Mama up and placed her in a wheelchair, her eyes shining with excitement. She opened the front door to greet the singers, who were not only bearing songs but also flowers and angels, symbols of love and blessings.

The magic of the moment was palpable. Mama's reaction was a sight to behold- a radiant smile of pure joy illuminated her face. In that fleeting instant, the years and she became the young girl she once was, reveling in the wonder of her special day.

Manianita, this cherished tradition of serenading birthday celebrants at the break of dawn, had brought a touch of enchantment to Mama's milestone birthday. It was a moment of connection, of love shared between generations, and a testament to the enduring spirit of our family.

Following the serenade, breakfast was served, and Mama was surrounded by family and the singers, all of whom had become part of this intimate celebration. The table was filled with love and laughter.

Finally, the time arrived for Mama to blow out her birthday cake. The room was hushed as the candles flickered, and with a heart full of wishes and love, she made her silent request to the universe. Then, as the gathered voices broke into song, she exhaled a breath that held a lifetime of hope and gratitude.

The Manianita serenade, with its ethereal beauty and heartfelt emotions, had set the tone for a day of celebration that would be marked by love, joy, and unity. In that magic moment, as the dawn welcomed the day, we were reminded of the timeless power of traditions and the enduring love that flowed through our family.

MONICA'S 97TH BIRTHDAY REUNION-DAY 1

Day 1 of our monumental 97th birthday reunion began with a sacred ritual that had become a cherished tradition in our family-a-Thanksgiving Mass at our beloved Catholic Church. The church, bathed in the soft morning light, was a place of reflection and gratitude where we gathered to offer thanks for the blessings that enriched our lives.

At around 8 am, family members from near and far congregated, filling the pews with the harmonious voices of prayer and song. The atmosphere was serene, a reminder that despite the passage of time and the physical distance that sometimes separated us, our faith and love for one another remained steadfast.

The Mass was a poignant celebration of not only Monica's life but also of the enduring legacy of love and faith that she had instilled in each of us. As the hymns swelled and incensed through the air, we were reminded of the profound connections that bound us- a connection that transcended generations and brought us together on this momentous occasion.

Following the Mass, we embarked on a journey that tugged at our hearts - a visit to the cemetery where our beloved departed rested. It was a solemn but poignant moment, a testament to the unbreakable bond that even death could not sever.

As we gathered by the gravesites, we offered prayers and shared stories about those who had gone before us. Their spirits seemed to linger in the gentle breeze, and their memories were etched in the very stones that marked their resting places. It was a reminder that the thread of family, woven through generations, extends beyond the confines of life itself.

Day 1 set the tone for our 97th birthday reunion—a tone of reflection, gratitude, and unity. It was a day that we acknowledged the roots from which we had sprung, paying homage to our faith and honoring those who had paved the way. And as we moved forward into the heart of our celebration, we carried with us the knowledge that our bonds, forged in love and faith, were as unyielding as time itself.

BEACH BLISS: CELEBRATING MONICA @97

After the heartfelt morning of reflection and remembrance, our 97th reunion transitioned into a vibrant celebration of life and togetherness—an unforgettable Beach Party at Big Sand Resort and Campground. This event, generously sponsored by the siblings, is a testament to the joyous spirit that permeated our family gatherings.

Upon arriving at the sun-kissed shores of Big Sand Resort Beach in our hometown, Moalboal, our hearts were lifted by the sights of tables and chairs spread across the fine, white sand, creating an inviting beachfront feast. The beach was the perfect canvas for our celebration, a wide expanse of pristine sand meeting the gently lapping waves of the sea.

Lunch was a sumptuous affair, with a catered spread that featured the iconic "Lechon" alongside an array of delectable Filipino dishes. Before indulging, Doc Jess, our beloved doctor of the family, led us in a heartfelt prayer, a moment of gratitude for the blessings of family and the nourishment before us.

Each family came dressed in their designated color theme, a tradition carried over from previous reunions, with shirts emblazoned with "Monica @97" on the front. The colors and vibrancy were a reflection of the unity and love that colored our celebration.

Family members of all ages, from the youngest children to the wisest elders, reveled in the festivities. Laughter filled the air as children built sandcastles and played by the shoreline while others captured the wide expanse of the white beach with their cameras.

As the sun reached its zenith, it was time for games to commence. Children squealed with delight as they participated in sack races while the adults engaged in spirited tug-of-war battles. Meanwhile, the young adults gathered for a playful game of "balloon passing," a testament to the camaraderie that flowed through our veins.

Amidst all the activity, Mama, seated in a wheelchair, radiated contentment under the warmth of the sun, sporting sunglasses and a hat. Her smile was a beacon of joy as she watched her family eat, swim, and engage in friendly competition. With an enthusiastic emcee keeping the spirit alive, every minute was a celebration of life.

The Beach Party continued through the afternoon, and the hours slipped away as we revealed the joy of being together. The sun dipped below the horizon, casting a warm glow over the beach, and our spirits remained high. It was a day of unity, laughter, and cherished memories- a fitting tribute to a woman whose love had brought us all together.

As the sundown was ready to start in the sky, we knew that this Beach party would forever be etched in our hearts, a chapter in the story of Monica's enduring legacy.

HARMONIOUS NIGHTFALL: KARAOKE AND TOGETHERNESS

As the sun dipped below the horizon, the Beach Party gave way to a harmonious nightfall that was equally spirited and heartwarming. The evening's centerpiece was a Karaoke setup in the front yard of my sister Jerry's house, complete with chairs and tables that welcomed guests to a relaxed dinner.

The dinner itself was simple yet comforting, a reflection of the unpretentious nature of our family gatherings. Each guest received a humble brown bag containing a delightful assortment of treats — empanadas, cookies, and various sweets that satisfied both the young and the young-at-heart. Refreshments included soda for the children and a selection of spirits for the young adults, creating an atmosphere that catered to all tastes.

As the night embraced us, the first notes of music filled the air, and the Karaoke came to life. Laughter and camaraderie infused the evening as family members, both young and old, took turns on the microphone. The yard became a dance floor, and the atmosphere was electric with the joyful sounds of singing and dancing.

The young generation, full of enthusiasm and boundless energy, showcased their singing talents while entertaining the older adults. Every note, every song, was a reminder of the love and unity that defined our family. In the background, the stars shone brightly, bearing witness to the cherished moments of togetherness.

As the night wore on and the moon ascended, the music continued to fill the air with laughter and merriment. But we were mindful of the late hour, and as a gesture of respect to our mother, who lived in the neighboring house, we decided to bring the evening to a close. The music gradually faded, and the chatter softened, a fitting conclusion to a day filled with love and celebration.

The echoes of that harmonious nightfall stayed with us, a reminder that our family gatherings were not just about grand gestures but also about simple moments of joy and togetherness. It was a night when we shared our voices and our hearts, creating memories that would linger long after the music had ceased.

BARRIO FIESTA EXTRAVAGANZA: A DAY OF GRANDCHILDREN'S LOVE

Day 2 of our monumental 2015 birthday celebration was a day that belonged to the grandchildren, a day filled with their meticulous planning and a grand vision. Their dedication and creativity were evident in every detail, from the vibrant decorations to the themed Photo Booth that awaited us.

The theme they chose was "Barrio Fiesta," a celebration of Filipino culture and cuisine. Grilled seafood, fresh and succulent, took center stage, and the dining experience was uniquely "boodle fight style." Food was laid out on long tables lined with generous banana leaves, and silverware was replaced by the warmth of our hands. As usual, the iconic Lechon was present, a symbol of abundance and festivity.

The early dinner was a sensory delight, accompanied by music playing softly in the background. Before we indulged in the delectable spread, each family member eagerly took their turn in the Photo Booth, capturing the vibrant spirit of the moment.

The front yard of my sister Jerry's house transformed into a colorful spectacle adorned with streamers and a sea of traditional Filipino attire, evoking the spirit of a barrio fiesta. It was a visual feast, a reflection of our rich cultural heritage.

As the dinner commenced, Doc Jesse, one of the grandchildren, led us in a heartfelt prayer, a moment to give thanks for the blessings of family and the abundance before us. It was a reminder that in the midst of grand celebrations, we remained rooted in our values and traditions.

Following dinner, the atmosphere shifted to one of spirited competition as Mona Liza took the lead in organizing family trivia games. Laughter and friendly banter filled the air, and the games brought us closer together, reinforcing the bonds that defined our family.

The evening continued with singing, dancing, and Karaoke as the night came alive with the vibrant energy of family members of all ages. Speeches were delivered, heartfelt tributes to Lola, the matriarch of our clan. However, when it was Lola's turn to speak, a hush fell over the crowd.

In her wheelchair, Lola's voice was soft, and her eyes glistened with tears of both joy and sadness. She spoke of her love for her family and the deep sense of contentment she felt. Then, unexpectedly, she uttered words that resonated in the hearts of all who were present. She expressed her belief that this might be her last reunion.

The revelation took us by surprise, and despite our efforts to offer comfort, the room fell silent, and tears welled in our eyes. It was a moment of mixed emotions, a reminder of the passage of time and the fragility of life. But it was also a moment that underscored the profound love that bound us together.

The night concluded with the younger generation celebrating, savoring the joy of the day with a touch of wine. It was a night that stirred a complex blend of emotions within us all—happiness, nostalgia, and a profound sense of love. In the midst of these emotions, we were reminded that our family's journey was a tapestry woven with threads of celebration and tears, laughter, and quiet reflection. It was a journey we would continue to cherish, whatever the future might hold.

In the tapestry of our family's history, the 97th birthday reunion of our beloved Mama stands as a chapter filled with vibrant colors and poignant emotions. It was a day and night of celebration, tradition, and heartfelt moments, where love and unity were the guiding stars.

As we bid farewell to this remarkable gathering, we do so with hearts brimming with gratitude and a tapestry of memories that will forever adorn our souls. It was a day when generations came together, sharing laughter and stories, singing and dancing, and, yes, shedding tears. It was a day of mixed emotions, where the joy of being together was tinged with the realization that time is a relentless river.

In those moments when Mama shared her heartfelt sentiments, we were reminded that our family's love transcends the years. It's a love that has been nurtured by her wisdom and care, a love that has sustained us through the seasons of life.

The 2015 birthday reunion was more than just an event; it was a reflection of our family's resilience, our unwavering bond, and the enduring legacy of love that our matriarch, Monica, bestowed upon us. It was a day when traditions were honored, culture celebrated, and, most importantly, family cherished.

As we close this chapter, we carry with us the memories of that day etched into our hearts like a beautiful melody. We remember the serenades at dawn, the boodle fight under the stars, and Mama's touching words that left us in quiet contemplation.

In the end, it was a celebration of a life well lived, a testament to the power of love and family. And even as we move forward into the unknown future, we know that the spirit of that day will continue to guide us, reminding us of the enduring bonds of family and the love that defines us.

The 2015 birthday reunion was a previous chapter in our family's story—a chapter that will forever shine as a beacon of hope, unity, and unwavering love. As we turn the page, we do so with hearts full of gratitude for the blessings of family and with the knowledge that our journey, like Mama's legacy, is boundless and everlasting.

THE HEARTBREAK OF BETRAYAL

*"Betrayal is a painful reminder that not everyone is worthy of our
trust., but should never dim the light of our authentic selves"*

Betrayal pierces the heart, leaving behind shards of trust and
echoes of disbelief. Yet in the face of such pain, resilience finds its
roots and healing begins with the courage to confront the truth.

In the twilight of her life, my mother, resilient and
independent, faced a betrayal that shattered her spirit. At 97 years
old, she found herself questioning the trust she had placed in those
around her, her once strong sense of security crumbling under the
weight of deceit.

It began with whispers of missing money, fleeting doubts
dismissed as forgetfulness of age. But as the truth unraveled, so too
did my mother's faith in those she loved. Hidden dollars and pesos,
carefully saved over a lifetime, vanished without a trace. The
realization left her reeling, grappling with a sense of loss and
betrayal that cut deeper than mere finances.

In her despair, she turned to her children, seeking solace in
their embrace. But even the bond of family could not ease the sting
of betrayal. Tears flowed freely as she confessed her fears and
pleaded for help, a once proud woman reduced to borrowing
money from her own children.

As we rallied around her, offering support and love, my sister
Mona embarked on a desperate search for the missing treasures -
not just the money and all her precious jewelries that were all
labeled with names of family members who will inherit, but the
pieces of my mother's identity stolen by deceit. Hour after hour,

she combed through drawers and closets, hoping to uncover the truth and restore some semblance of peace to our shattered family.

Yet, despite our efforts, the wounds of betrayal ran deep. The caregiver, entrusted with my mother's care and confidence, vanished without a trace, leaving behind a void that could not be filled. And though we sought justice and closure, the scars of betrayal lingered casting a shadow over our final reunion.

In the end, it was a loss that transcended mere possessions. It was a loss of trust, of faith, of the unwavering belief that love and family could conquer all. And as we said our final goodbyes to my beloved mother, I couldn't help but wonder - how do you mend a broken heart?

This incident, painful though it may be to revisit, serves as a poignant reminder of the fragility of trust and the enduring power of love. And as I share my mother's story with the world, I do not dwell on the pain of the past, but to honor her legacy of resilience, compassion, and unwavering faith in the face of adversity.

CHAPTER 35
JOURNEY THROUGH LOSS AND HOMECOMING: A SON'S FAREWELL AND A MOTHER'S PEACEFUL DEPARTURE

"In the depth of sorrow, we find strength. In the face of loss, we discover resilience. And in the embrace of home, we find peace."

In the tapestry of our family's life, there are chapters that shine with joy and chapters that are shaded by sorrow. This chapter, one of the latter, delves into a period of profound loss and trials that tested the strength of our bonds.

It begins with the story of my brother, Fred, a beloved companion to our mother, Monica. Theirs was a unique bond, a partnership that brought comfort and companionship to both of their lives. In the twilight years, as Fred's health became fragile, he became Mama's steadfast driver and confidante. Together, they navigated the city, enjoyed meals at their favorite restaurants, and cherished each moment of their outings.

But the fragility of life, so often concealed beneath the veil of daily routines, caught us by surprise in September 2015. Fred's health took a sharp turn, and within a week, he had left this world, leaving a void in our hearts that could have never been filled.

Grief descended upon our family, casting a shadow that stretched across continents. Those of us in the United States hastily made plans to return home for the funeral, to be by Mama's side, and to mourn the loss of a dear brother. Little did we know that the trials that awaited us would be even more daunting.

As we prepared to face the inevitable sorrow, we found ourselves confronted with another harsh reality. Mama, who had already borne the weight of her own grief, fell seriously ill. Her strength waned, and it became evident that her own health was teetering on the edge of uncertainty. Thus began a heart-wrenching journey that would test our resilience, our faith, and our capacity to confront the darkest moments of life. In this chapter, we will walk this challenging path together, recounting the struggles, the tears, and the moments of grace that carried us through.

It is a chapter marked by vulnerability, by the stark realities of illness and loss, but also by the enduring love that binds us as a family. It is a chapter that reveals the profound depths of our relationship and the strength we discover when faced with life's most difficult trials. This is the story of Fred, of Mama, and of our family's unwavering resilience in the face of adversity.

A MOTHER'S INTUITION

In the dimly lit room, where grief and anticipation intertwined, an unforgettable moment unfolded. It was the time of my brother Fred's passing, a somber occasion that cast a past over our hearts. But amidst the sorrow, a small yet profound incident transpired that would forever resonate in our memories.

As my brother's wife was at his bedside, where his life was quietly slipping away, my mother was in her own room at home, her eyes closed in restless sleep. And then, in the fragile stillness, something extraordinary happened. My mother, seemingly lost in the realm of dreams, stirred. She murmured softly, her voice a mere whisper, but her words carried a weight that left us breathless. With her hand gently raised, she spoke the name that held so much meaning for all of us at that moment.

"Fred, wait for me," she uttered, her words hanging in the air like a sacred promise.

It was as if, even in her slumber, my mother possessed an intuition that transcended the boundaries of the earthly. In her dreams, she reached out to my brother, extending an unseen hand, a gesture of love and connection that stretched across the chasm between his life and the next.

In that poignant moment, we were reminded of the profound bond that had existed between them, a connection that neither time nor distance could diminish. It was a testament to a mother's unwavering love and a son's enduring presence in her heart.

THE DIFFICULT JOURNEY TO MODERN CARE

As we returned to bid a final farewell to my brother Fred, we carried the weight of sorrow in our hearts. But little did we know that our arrival would unveil a series of unexpected challenges, thrusting us into the throes of uncertainty and fear.

As the family came together to make preparations for my brother's funeral, there was an underlying sense of anxiety. It was not just the loss of Fred that weighed heavily upon us; it was also the deteriorating health of our beloved mother, Monica. Her illness had been shrouded in a cloud of mystery and unpredictability.

After her initial admission to the old community hospital in Cebu City, Mama's words echoed with clarity, her resolve unwavering despite her fragility; "Get me out of here. I do not like this old and outdated hospital. Please transfer me to Perpetual Succour Hospital. I want to stay there because it has modern facilities."

Her plea was a testament to her strength and her desire for the best care possible, and it presented us with a formidable challenge. The Perpetual Succour Hospital was the modern medical facility she sought, but it was also known for its high demand and limited availability. Securing a bed felt like an arduous uphill battle.

Hours stretched into eternity as we negotiated tirelessly, calling on every connection we had, seeking that elusive vacancy. After six hours of persistence, and finally, a glimmer of hope emerged. We received the news: a bed had become available. It was a moment of relief, tinged with anxiety for what lay ahead.

Mama was swiftly transferred to the Perpetual Succour Hospital's emergency room, where stakes were at their highest. Here, in those tense hours, we faced the true gravity of her condition. Her body had succumbed to a cardiac rhythm that was erratic and dangerous.

For five harrowing hours in the ER, we watched as the medical team worked tirelessly to revive her not once but three times. The room was filled with the sounds of medical equipment and hushed voices and through it all. I kept touching and calling her name, willing her to stay with us.

Miraculously, her eyes opened, and she responded to my voice, defying the odds and displaying a tenacity that was characteristic of her spirit. In those agonizing moments, the boundary between life and the unknown seemed paper thin.

Finally, a sense of relief washed over us as Mama was transferred to the Intensive Care Unit (ICU). It was there that she found comfort, stability, and the vigilant care she needed. Monitors beeped rhythmically, offering reassurance that her condition was being closely watched.

This was the beginning of an arduous journey in the ICU, where Mama would continue to fight against the ravages of illness. It was a journey that would test our family's resilience, our faith, and our capacity to confront the darkest moments of life. In the pages that follow, we will walk alongside Mama as she navigates the uncertain path of her medical journey, seeking not just modern care but also hope and healing.

Navigating the ICU: A Family's Vigil

As we faced the daunting reality of Mama's critical condition in the ICU of Perpetual Succour Hospital, our family's world seemed to hang in a precarious balance. We were torn between the urgent need to attend my brother's funeral in Moalboal, our hometown, and the unwavering commitment to be by Mama's side during her time of need.

It was a time of heart-wrenching decisions. With heavy hearts, we left Mama in the capable hands of the medical team in Cebu City and embarked on the journey back to Moalboal to lay my brother Fred to rest. It was a funeral marked not just by sorrow but also by the bittersweet knowledge that we were unable to fully grieve our loss while Mama's own health teetered on the edge.

In the midst of our mourning, we received word that my sisters, brother, and his daughter, who had been on their way home from the United States, were drawing near. Additionally, my children and nieces, whose vacation requests had been granted, were preparing to make the long journey back to the Philippines to be with Mama. Each arrival brought with it a renewed sense of hope and solidarity.

Day after day, family members arrive at the hospital to visit Mama in the ICU. We took turns ensuring that she was never alone, even in the sterile and sometimes intimidating environment of the intensive care unit, yet this system did not align with Mama's wishes.

His heart's desire was to be in a regular room, surrounded by all family members. She longed for the warmth and comfort of our presence as we did for her. However, the severity of her condition necessitated the constant monitoring that only the ICU could provide.

In this challenging juncture, my nephew, Jessie, a doctor himself, stepped forward as an advocate for Mama. He tirelessly negotiated with the medical team in the ICU, pleading for Mama's case and emphasizing the importance of her family's presence in her healing process.

After much deliberation and heartfelt conversations, a breakthrough came. The medical team agreed to allow Mama to move to a regular room under one condition: she had to be continuously monitored. We assured the medical team that my nephew, Dr. Jess, Hazel, and Karla (both nurses), who had just arrived from the United States, would monitor my mother continuously. It was a compromise that Mama gladly accepted, and the weight of our collective presence became her beacon of strength.

In a remarkable turn of events, Mama's wishes were granted for the second time. As she settled into her new room after a challenging transfer, surrounded by the love and care of her family, a spark of happiness returned to her eyes. It was a testament to the power of love and determination, a testament to the unwavering bond that held our family together even in the face of adversity.

This chapter marked a pivotal moment in Mama's journey, one where her family's resilience and unity became an integral part of her healing process. In the pages following, we will accompany Mama through the challenges and triumphs of her hospital stay, a journey that will test our faith, our patience, and our capacity to be there for each other.

SURROUNDED BY LOVE: MAMA'S JOURNEY IN A REGULAR ROOM

The moment Mama was transferred to a regular room, her wish was granted-she was finally surrounded by all her family and loved ones. She lay in bed, frail and weak, her breathing labored, while my nephew Doc Jesse and my niece Hazel, alongside my daughter, Karla, who are competent nurses, continually monitored her vital signs.

In that room, emotions ran high. All of us siblings gathered around her, offering prayers and shedding tears as we witnessed her struggle. Mama drifted in and out of consciousness, and with each passing moment, we feared that it might be her final goodbye. Her strength wavered, but her spirit remained resilient.

As the clock struck midnight, we couldn't help but wonder if she was waiting for something or someone. And then, it became clear. My son Jerome, the last family member to arrive from the US, entered the room. Mama is weak but still aware, recognizes him, and simply acknowledges his presence with a loving gaze.

We knew that Mama's time with us was limited, and she longed to connect with those who couldn't be physically present. With trembling hands, we put our sister, Judith, who unfortunately couldn't make the journey home, on a phone call with Mama. It was a heart-wrenching conversation filled with tears and emotional exchanges. Even in her weakened state, Mama's love and longing transcended the distance that separated them.

But then, as if granting us all a moment of respite, Mama's demeanor shifted. She conveyed through her gestures that she was ready to go, that she had made peace with what lay ahead. And with that, she closed her eyes and drifted off to sleep.

A priest had already administered the last rites of sacrament, offering her solace and spiritual comfort. The room, once filled with tears and prayers, now held a different kind of atmosphere. It was one of profound sorrow, but also a celebration, for Mama's peaceful departure had been witnessed by those who loved her most.

As dawn broke, Mama remained calm. Her monitored vital signs were stable, and her family, exhausted and emotionally drained, left her in the capable hands of our family's medical team. We hoped that the peace she had found in her sleep would continue.

Yet, before she had drifted off, Mama had uttered words that tugged at our hearts. She had asked to go home—a plea to return to her beloved house in Moalboal, a place filled with memories, love, and a lifetime of moments.

In the days that followed, we would continue to watch over Mama, bearing witness to her journey as she navigated the uncertain path that lay ahead. It was a journey marked by love, longing, and the resilience of a family united by a profound bond.

A JOURNEY TO HOME, A JOURNEY TO PEACE

The following morning brought with it an unexpected surprise, one that filled our hearts with both hope and challenge. We found

Mama, still very frail and weak but now a little more awake. Her voice was feeble, and she kept muttering a single fervent desire: "I want to go home."

We gathered around her bedside, trying to gently explain that there was no ambulance available to make the journey from the city to Moalboal, our hometown, where Mama so desperately wished to be. We explored every avenue, reaching out to various channels, seeking a way to fulfill her fervent request.

In response, Mama's voice, though irritated and weakened, held a note of determination. "There are plenty of ambulances," she asserted. It was a sentiment that both surprised and inspired us. Her unwavering resolve spoke to a strength that transcended her physical fragility.

Driven by her heartfelt plea, we set out to make her wish a reality. My late brother Alex took on the mission. He made the arduous journey from the city to Moalboal, where he negotiated with the local medical team stationed there. It was a delicate and intricate process, filled with logistical challenges but fueled by the urgency of Mama's longing.

Finally, after countless efforts and tireless negotiations, we received the news we had been waiting for: the use of the Moalboal ambulance had been approved. The wheels of this plan, set in motion by our mother's fervent desire, were now in motion.

With meticulous care and attention, arrangements were made to ensure Mama's comfort during the journey, as well as to equip the ambulance with the necessary medical emergency equipment. Every detail was considered to ensure her safety and well-being.

And so, with the afternoon sun beginning to set, Mama embarked on a journey that was both a return to her beloved home and a passage toward peace. She was accompanied by her private nurse and devoted caregiver, the very individuals who tirelessly cared for her throughout her hospital stay.

As the ambulance set out on the road from the city to Moalboal, Mama closed her eyes. In those quiet moments, she whispered to her companion, urging them to pray the rosary. It was a gesture of faith and solace, a reflection of her unwavering spirit even in the midst of such a profound transition.

The journey was not just a physical one; it was a testament to the power of a mother's love and the lengths to which a family would go to fulfill her deepest wishes. It was a journey home, and for Mama, it was a journey toward the peace she had longed for.

THE HOMECOMING AND THE FINAL PEACE

As Mama was finally home, nestled in the comfort of her own bed, a profound sense of peace seemed to envelop her. Despite her eyes remaining closed, her breathing had returned to a gentle, rhythmic cadence. It was as if the very act of being in her familial surroundings had granted her solace.

In those precious moments, we were acutely aware of the saying that hearing is often the last sense to fade. So, we continued to speak to her, our words filled with love and reassurance. We took turns sharing stories, reminiscing about cherished memories, and offering words of comfort. It was our way of letting her know that she was not alone and that we were there with her every step of the way.

With the weight of the past days finally lifted, we retreated to our own beds, allowing ourselves the rest we desperately needed. A private nurse, ever vigilant, remained by Mama's side, monitoring her vital signs and ensuring her comfort throughout the night.

As the clock approached 4 a.m., a gentle urge pulled me from my sleep. I found myself drawn to Mama's bedside once more, a quiet presence in the stillness of the night. I reached out to her, speaking softly and tenderly. To my surprise and solace, she responded with a nod, a silent acknowledgement of our connection.

The rest of the night passed with a sense of serenity that we had not felt in a day. Mama slept peacefully, breathing a steady lullaby that echoed through the room. When the morning light filtered through the windows, a sense of calm washed over the room.

It was then that my sister-in-law, Amai, arrived. She had been unable to visit Mama in the hospital during those tumultuous days, as she had been tirelessly arranging the funeral for my late brother, Fred. Amai's presence was a balm to our hearts. She prayed, sang, and spoke softly to Mama, assuring her that everything would be alright, that there is no need to worry. Amai knew just how deeply Mama loved and cared for my brother, and her words carried the weight of that shared love.

Minutes after Amai left, the private nurse summoned us, her face reflecting the somber truth that we had been preparing for. Mama's vital signs were steadily declining, a clear indication that her journey was nearing its end. It was then that we knew who she was waiting for before her final peaceful departure.

With a heavy but resigned heart, we gathered all the family members who were ready to go to work that morning. We surrounded Mama, forming a protective circle of love and support. There were no more tears, no more sobs. Instead, we prayed together, our voices rising in unison.

My nephew, Jesse, an MD, took note of the exact time as we stood witness to Mama's final moments. In that sacred space, as she took her last breath, there was a profound sense of peace. We knew that she had found her way home, that she was free from pain, and that she was at rest.

The room, once filled with the heavy weight of sorrow, now held a different kind of presence. It was one of reverence, of a life well lived, and a love that endured beyond the boundaries of time. We gathered around her, our hands linked in a final farewell, a whispered thank you, and a profound sense of gratitude for having been part of her extraordinary journey.

As we took our leave, we knew that Mama, at 97 years old, had finally found the eternal peace she had been seeking. Though the ache of her absence would linger, the legacy of her love and strength would live in our hearts, forever guiding us on our own journeys of love and resilience.

DESIGNING HER FINAL RESTING PLACE

As my mother's final days approached, she displayed a remarkable sense of grace and foresight. Ever the meticulous planner, she had already taken steps to ensure that her burial reflected her own wishes and her deep connection to our family's history.

Years before passing, she had carefully chosen a burial vault and location. Her decision was deliberate: she wanted to rest beside my father, her beloved husband, in the same private lot we had in our hometown cemetery. This choice was a testament to the enduring love they shared and their desire to be together even in eternity.

CONCLUSION: A FINAL ACT OF CONTROL

In the end, as we stood witness to Mama's final moments, it became abundantly clear that she had not lost control; she had merely redefined it. Just as she had taken command of raising her twelve children single-handedly after our father's untimely departure, she had now taken control of her own journey toward the inevitable.

Even in her most fragile moments, Mama remained steadfast in her unwavering spirit. She had issued a fervent request and, through sheer determination, had ensured it was granted. Her longing to return home, to the place filled with memories and love, was not just a plea; it was a final assertion of her will, a testament to the strength that had defined her life.

Throughout her journey, Mama taught us the profound meaning of love and resilience. She had endured countless sacrifices and hardships, raising us with unwavering dedication. Her love had been unconditional, her care boundless, and her spirit unyielding.

As she departed this world, it was with the knowledge that she was surrounded by love, that her family stood by her side, and that we were grateful beyond measure for all the sacrifices she had made. Her legacy of unconditional love would live on in us, a beacon guiding our lives and illuminating our paths.

In her final act of control, Mama had orchestrated her departure with grace and dignity. She had left knowing that the love she had poured into us had taken root, blossoming into an enduring legacy that would forever define our family.

As we bid her farewell, we did so with heavy hearts but also with profound gratitude for having shared in her remarkable journey. Mama may have left this earthly realm, but her love and strength would remain etched in our hearts, guiding us through the chapters of our lives yet to be written. In her final moments, She showed that love and control don't have to be separate; they can work together in a harmonious dance, leaving behind a legacy that will endure for generations.

CHAPTER 36
MOTHER'S LEGACY: UNVEILING WISDOM AND HIDDEN TREASURES

"Some gifts you hold in your hand; some you hold in your heart."

In the quiet corners of our lives, where memories and legacies reside, there exists a space where wisdom and treasures intermingle. It is in this sacred space that we uncover the essence of those who came before us, leaving behind a roadmap for our own journey.

This chapter is a journey into the heart of discovery-discovery of both tangible riches and tangible pearls of wisdom. It is a testament to the enduring influence of a mother who raised twelve children with unparalleled strength and resilience. Here, we delve into the treasure trove she left behind, not only in the form of material legacy but also in the form of profound guidance for life's twists and turns.

As we embark on this voyage, we explore the pages of her advice, her reflections on life's greatest rewards, and the scriptures that illuminate her path. Through her own words, we gain insight into the values that shaped her journey and the principles she wished to impact her family.

But this chapter is more than a mere exploration of possessions or philosophies. It is a celebration of a well-lived and profound impact one person can have on those they touch. It is an acknowledgement of the treasures she entrusted to our care and the wisdom she bequeathed to guide our steps.

In the pages that follow, we invite you to join us on the journey of unveiling—a journey into the heart of a mother's legacy, where wisdom and treasures coalesce, forever echoing in the corridors of our lives.

THE HIDDEN TREASURES

Amid the somber task of clearing my mother's room and organizing after her passing, we stumbled upon a treasure trove of memories hidden in plain sight. As we carefully went through her personal items, we came across a small little book tucked away in a drawer, each page filled with her handwritten words.

It was her diary testament to her innermost thoughts, dreams, and emotions, which she kept hidden away from prying eyes for decades. The discovery felt like tumbling upon a secret passage to her heart, a portal to the depths of her soul that she had chosen to share only with the pages of this diary.

With a sense of reverence, we gathered as a family and began to read the diary together. Each entry revealed a facet of her life — her joys, her sorrows, her hopes, her wisdom, and her fears. Her words painted a vivid portrait of the woman behind the roles of mother and matriarch. We saw her through the lens of her own reflections, and it was a revelation.

The diary was a chronicle of her journey, written in her own hand, in her own words. It captured moments of triumph and moments of doubt, the everyday joys of life, her faith, and the quiet moments of introspection. Reading her diary was like taking a guided tour through the tapestry of her life, with every entry a thread that added depth and color to the narratives.

As we turned the pages, we realized the profound impact her diary had on us. It was as though she was speaking to us from beyond the veil, imparting wisdom, sharing her experiences, and reminding us of the values she held dear. It was a gift. A legacy of love and self-reflection- that she had left behind.

A Glimpse into Mama's Heart and Wisdom:

In these sections, I invite you to join me on a journey through the intimate pages of Mama's diary. These diary entries offer a glimpse into the heart and soul of a woman who raised twelve children with love, courage, and an unshakable resolve.

Through these excerpts, we will share in her joys, empathize with her sorrows, and draw inspiration from the wisdom she left behind. It is my hope that by revealing these intimate words, we can keep her memory alive and pass down the lessons she learned to future generations.

So, let us embark on this poignant journey as we listen to Mama's voice from the past, echoing the ensuing values and love that continue to shape our lives.

Excerpts from Mother's Diary

_ "Life's Greatest Rewards for Me: 'In my life's struggle as both a father and a mother, the Good Lord keeps watch over me as I come and go to manage my great responsibility of taking care of my children in times of fear and uncertainty. At the end of life's difficulties, I should say, "I reached the end of the rainbow and found the pot of gold "as life's greatest reward for me. Thank You, Lord!! I Praise You !!I love You!!" "_Happiest Time of my Life: I experienced many happy moments of my life, but today at the age of 89 yrs. old (a few months more to 90 yrs. old,) is the happiest time of my life, "Praise the Lord" Why? Because I am surrounded by ambitious, hardworking, successful members of EMMO Sandalo Clan which is composed of doctors, nurses, engineers, business analysts, teachers, managers, pharmacists, computer engineers and many more. And of course the regular financial support of Thelma and Mona Liza."

"_Life's Greatest Gifts for Me: Life's greatest gift for me is my long life and good health that God gives me. Another greatest gift that life gives me is my "life's devotions and life's sacrifices, with one thought, one hope, one feeling that my children will grow up healthy and strong, free from evil habits and able to provide themselves."

"The saddest time of my life is during and after the death of my beloved partner (Nanong) who passed away on Nov. 1, 1968. After his untimely death, I began to face the most difficult challenges."

"The most fascinating places I visited are Las Vegas, Florida and Disneyland. If I become young again by magic (God willing) I'll go back to Las Vegas."

"If I could keep only one family photo, it would be a family photo of the Grand Reunion of the EMMO clan in 1995. This memorable affair portrays the love and strong desire to be together again. This grand affair was held in Cebu Plaza."

WORDS OF WISDOM AND SPIRITUAL GUIDANCE:

In the quiet corners of my mother's heart, she held precious gems—nuggets of wisdom, glimpses of her deepest desires, and the guiding light of her faith. These treasures, like the diary we uncovered, revealed a mother layer of her essence. In this section, we explore the pages of her advice, the reflections on life's greatest rewards, and the scriptures that held a special place in her heart.

In her own words, she left behind a legacy of guidance, a testament to the values that shaped her journey. As we delve into her thoughts, we discover the essence of the woman we knew and loved and perhaps even uncover new facets of her character.

EXCERPTS FROM MOTHER'S DIARY

"-Religion played a significant role in my life. It taught me about God, and His Creation, His wondrous story, our Salvation, All His Great Things He had done and many more about His Greatness."

SCRIPTURES: MOTHER'S SPIRITUAL GUIDANCE AND INSPIRATION

"__Romans 12:19 Dearly beloved, avenge not yourselves, but rather give place unto wrath: for it is written, Vengeance is mine; I will repay saith the Lord.

__Romans 12:19

"So what must we do when someone offends us? We must continue to be good and let God handle. Vengeance in His perfect time and way."

__James 1:22-23

But be ye doers of the word, and not hearers only, deceiving your own selves. For if any be a hearer of the word, and not a doer, he is like unto a man beholding his natural face in a glass.

"And remember, it is a message to obey, not just to listen to. If you do not obey, you are only fooling yourself. Teach by example, and do what you teach."

__2 Corinthians 9: 6

But this I say, He which soweth sparingly shall also reap sparingly, and he which soweth bountifully shall also reap bountifully.

"Remember this farmer who plants only a few seeds will get a small crop. But the one who plants generously will get a generous crop."

Each page we turn is a conversation with her- a conversation that transcends time and space. Her advice serves as a compass, her reflections on life's rewards echo in our hearts, and the scriptures she cherished offer solace and inspiration.

Words of Wisdom: (Excerpts from Mama's Diary)

"Love and Honor your parents."

"A Loving Touch Can Turn a life around."

"Life is what you make it."

What I hope my children learn from me are:

Can be trusted in words and in deeds.

Not to spend more than what you earn.

Lend a helping hand to those who are in dire need."

Lazy people want much but get little, but those who work hard will prosper and be satisfied."

As we navigate the wisdom she left behind, let us honor her memory and the enduring impact of her words. For in her guidance, we find not just a testament to her life but a roadmap for our own.

REFLECTIONS

As I read through the intimate pages of Mama's diary. I couldn't help but be transported back in time to moments both joyous and challenging, all seen through her eyes. Her words were like a bridge connecting me to her world. Allowing me to glimpse the depths of her heart and the resilience of her spirit.

One recurring theme in Mama's diary was her unwavering faith. Her favorite scriptures were more than mere words; they were guiding stars that illuminated her path through life's darkest nights. Her faith was a beacon of hope, a constant source of strength that carried her through trials and tribulations. It was evident in her unwavering trust that God's plan was unfolding, even when life's circumstances seemed insurmountable.

As I read her diary, I realized that Mama's legacy extended far beyond her. Her faith and wisdom were not confined to the pages but lived on in each of her children, grandchildren, and even great-grandchildren. Her capacity to love had woven our family together, creating a tapestry of warmth and support that stretched across generations.

In closing, Mama's diary was not just a collection of thoughts; it was a testament to a life well-lived, a love well-shared, and a faith unwavering in the face of adversity. Her words continue to guide and inspire us, reminding us of the immeasurable gift we had in her. Mama's hidden treasure, her diary, now serves as a beacon of light, illuminating our path as we carry forward her legacy of love, wisdom, and faith.

Epilogue

A Life Remembered: Monica An Unforgettable Portrait

"When we lose someone we love; we must learn not to live without them but to live with the love they left behind."

In the final pages of this memoir, we come full circle to celebrate a life that defied the odds, a life filled with faith, unwavering love, and an unyielding spirit. Monica's journey, as recounted in these pages, is a testament to the resilience of the human soul and the power of a mother's love.

As we reflect on her story, we are reminded of the countless lives she touched, not only as a mother to her twelve children but as a beloved sister, aunt, cousin, and friend. Her warmth, generosity, and boundless love were qualities that endeared her to all who knew her.

But the impact of her life extended far beyond her immediate family. In the sections that follow, we will hear the heartfelt tributes of in-laws and cousins, those who shared in the privilege of knowing and loving Monica. Their words offer a glimpse into the profound influence she had on the lives of many, the indelible mark she left on their hearts.

In this collection of testimonials, we celebrate the life and legacy of a woman whose kindness, strength, and grace left an indelible mark on all who crossed her path. As I embark on this chapter of her memoir, I find myself humbled by the wealth of memories, stories, and anecdotes shared by cousins, friends, and loved ones who were touched by her presence.

We will journey through time, revisiting the moments of love, joy and wisdom that define Monica's life. Through the words of those who cherished her, we honor a well-lived spirit that continues to inspire us all. Welcome to "Remembering Monica: An Unforgettable Portrait," a chapter that brings together the voices of those whose lives were forever touched by her extraordinary presence.

MEMORIES AND TRIBUTES:

"Summer vacations were my favorite time of the year. It was an opportunity to visit Moalboal, my father's hometown and my birthplace and I eagerly anticipated each year. My sister and I would stay at Auntie Moning's house, and I cherish the moments spent with her and my cousins. Auntie Moning was a unique and cherished member of our family.

During our stay, she personally selected fresh food from the market to prepare delicious meals. We engaged in various outdoor activities, from walks in the plaza to beach outings. Evenings were spent sharing stories, some about our family's history and others about life's struggles. Auntie's warmth and the togetherness of those moments strengthened our bond with her family.

During the Holy Week, we immersed ourselves in church traditions, including processions. The highlight of our vacation was the town's grand fiesta celebration.

Auntie worked tirelessly to prepare an array of dishes for everyone to enjoy. In the evening, she transformed into the life of the town's grand fiesta evening dance, showcasing her excellent dance moves with my father and her nephews.

Auntie was not just a great teacher; she was also a diligent, strict, and loving mother who cared for her 12 children and then some. Auntie was my father's favorite sister.

Her deep respect for her father mirrored my father's traits of intelligence, generosity, and strictness.

One of my most cherished memories is the unexpected call she made to me a few years ago before her passing, simply because she missed me. That's the Auntie I hold dear in my heart."

-Victoria Babiera Neri (cousin)

"Lola Moning, as we affectionately called her, held a special place in our hearts. She was not just our grandmother's (Petronila) younger sister; she was a beloved member of our family. Lola Moning's love and care knew no bounds, extending to us in the same way she treated her own children and grandchildren.

During her visits to Cape Coral, Florida, she left an indelible mark on us with her famous Danish cookies, known for their delightful buttery flavor. Her stay at our parents' house was filled with moments we cherish, like the time she taught us the art of making pandesal, ensaymada (sweet bread), and those delectable buttery cookies.

Whenever we journeyed to Moalboal, she warmly welcomed us to her home for dinner. Her loving presence and captivating stories, including the secret to her youthful spirit, left an enduring impression on all of us."

-Sandy Jumalon Fay (Grandniece)

"So glad and deeply touched that my dearest Tiya (Aunt) Moning took time to join us and witnessed our vows. It is through your Mom that I learned the true meaning of perseverance, which, according to her, is the master key to anything, especially in marriage. I value the lesson more than I can explain. Tiya Moning is an inspiration and genuine teacher with PhD in human survival."

-Vellie Dietrich Hall (Cousin)

"I had the privilege of meeting Mama Moning in Moalboal during Tom's (nephew) baptism, where I served as one of Tom's godmothers. Our paths crossed again during the "Pamanhikan" in Valladolid, Carcar, a special tradition of asking for my hand in marriage to Fred. The third meeting took place on our wedding day, and from then on, I had the chance to interact with Mama Moning on several occasions in different places across Cebu.

Mama Moning was a remarkable and determined person. Her children were her guiding light, and she always ensured that her presence and wisdom often conveyed through her thoughts, were taken to heart. It's worth noting that I had the privilege of being the last family member to bid farewell to Mama Moning, and my last memory of her was on the morning of October 6,2015, in Moalboal. Over the course of 33 years, I'm proud to say that I developed a strong and positive relationship with my mother-in-law.

-Amai Sandalo (Sister-in-law)

"It is truly an honor to write about a remarkable woman. Auntie Moning, as I fondly called her, was not just an aunt but my closest and dearest relative during my formative years. She held a special place in my father's heart as his favorite sibling.

Every vacation, my sister and I eagerly anticipated our visits to Moalboal, where we would stay in Auntie Moning's welcoming home. Those times were the highlight of our childhood, surrounded by the warmth and love of Auntie Moning and her children.

Auntie Moning was not only hospitable but also a loving and caring mother to her 12 children, especially after the loss of Uncle Nanong. Her infectious smile, hearty laughter, and her timeless beauty left an indelible mark on all who knew her. One memory that stands out is our shared birthdays, hers on May 4 and mine just three days after. It's a bond I cherish.

Though life took me far from Moalboal for some time, I eventually returned to the Philippines for medical missions. Seeing Auntie Moning's clear mind and enduring memory until her passing was truly inspiring. I deeply admire her resilience and

strength. Auntie, you will always have a special place in my heart. I believe you are now rejoined with your beloved children and Uncle in heaven. I love you, Auntie, and may you find eternal happiness."

-Lagrimas Sadorra M.D. (Cousin)

"Aunt Moning, or Seniora Monica, as I affectionately address her, was truly a remarkable woman. Her strength and unwavering character left a lasting impression on me. I was deeply impressed by her resilience in the face of life's challenges, especially as she single-handedly raised her children to become responsible adults.

Her warm and welcoming smile, coupled with her gracious hospitality during our visits to Moalboal, will forever remain etched in my memory."

-Marian Romea (Distant Cousin)

"I always looked forward to the moments when Mama Moning visited our home in Vegas. Her cooking was simply exceptional, and every meal she prepared was a delightful feast for the senses. Beyond her culinary talents, she shared her remarkable stories of her experiences during World War II, and I shared my own military experience during the Vietnam War. She was an extraordinary woman, filled with strength and wisdom.

-Hillis E. Golden (husband)

"Today, I am filled with happiness and pride as I fondly remember a remarkable woman who graced this world for 97 years. Mama Moning, as we affectionately called her, was not just a loving mother to her 12 children but also a beacon of warmth and kindness to her extended family, including myself. Her exceptional qualities and unwavering commitment to strong family bonds ensured that our interactions with her were always filled with love, understanding and support.

The passage of time saw her children grow to establish their own families, and sometimes, life's circumstances led them away from the nest. This natural progression often brought emotional longing for reunions, but the constraints of time, distance, and logistics made it challenging. Despite these challenges, Mama Moning's enduring love and grace were a constant source of comfort.

Today, we extend our heartfelt gratitude to our dear Lord for the countless blessings and graces bestowed upon our family. We remember and cherish the beautiful memories, unwavering support, and boundless love that Mama Moning shared with us. As we gather in joyful reunion, we also honor her memory, confident that her strong and gentle soul now rests in eternal peace with the Lord.

May this coming reunion be a testament to the enduring strength of the Sandalo family, and may God's continued guidance and protection light our path in the journey ahead. God bless us all.

-Bonifacio Villanueva Ed. D (Brother -in-Law)

"My mother-in-law was an incredible woman who embodied courage, discipline, and determination. These qualities were essential for her as she raised and educated 12 children as a young widow. Despite coming from different eras, we shared many common values. We both grew up in strict households, believed in the importance of education, followed our Roman Catholic faith devoutly, upheld strong moral values, and knew that discipline was crucial in raising children.

During the early years of my marriage to her son, Emiliano Jr. (a.k.a. Juhn) and I, we had the privilege of spending time with her. Even though these moments were brief, they left a lasting impact. I remembered how she cooked for us, and that's how I learned to make her famous Moalboal fried chicken, a dish Juhn fondly calls "Mama's Fried Chicken."

One of my cherished memories is from my birthday while we were living in Glendale. She brought me a plant and kept it hidden until my special day. The plant still thrives today on my kitchen window sill, serving as a daily reminder of her.

During the challenging years when Juhn and I were busy with our careers and raising our two young daughters, Mama came to stay with us for a short time to lend her support as we desperately needed from our family members. Her presence during those

315

demanding times was a godsend, and with her help and God's grace, we managed to overcome the obstacles.

In her later years, when we visited Moalboal on vacation, we would spend time at her home, engaging in pleasant conversations. She often reminisced about her travels across America and the people she had met. We also invite her to our vacation house, creating cherished memories together. In 2010, she graced us with her presence at the blessing of our vacation house, where she witnessed many of Juhn's dreams come to fruition.

These memories are a testament to her love, support, and the deep bond we shared. Mama Moning's influence will forever be a part of our lives, reminding us of her unwavering love and wisdom."

I want to share a bit of trivia that occurred many years ago:

Many years before Juhn and I were born, Mama Moning had already heard about our family, the Jakosalem family from the town of Dumanjug and the Calderon family from the town of Samboan, all neighboring towns of Moalboal. Mama Moning once shared with me that as a young 16-year-old girl, she would observe from a distance as my maternal grandmother stepped out of her father's Berlina car when they came to buy fish at the market. Lola Beyay frequently visited Moalboal with her father to select the finest fish, as Moalboal was renowned for its excellent fish selection.

Many, many years ago, my aunt opened the first rural bank in the town of Dumanjug, and Lola Beyay managed it for her daughter. One of her customers applying for a loan happened to be Mama Moning. At that time, Juhn, who was unmarried and working in America, extended his assistance to help Mama Moning pay off that loan.

Little did he know that this act of kindness would eventually lead to his marriage to the granddaughter of Dorothea, a remarkable connection that transcends generations.

Call it synchronicity, coincidence, destiny, or divine intervention on how Juhn and I had eventually crossed paths in California, which is oceans away from Cebu, Philippines. As Mama Moning looks down from above, she would be very pleased at the legacy she left behind.

Eternal rest grant unto Mama Moning, Oh Lord, and let perpetual light shine upon her. May she rest in peace. Amen.

-Genevieve Gobuyan Sandalo (sister-in-law)

An in-law Perspective:

"On that chilly December 24th in 2005, the air in our Filipino-style Christmas Eve party was filled with the rich aroma of lechon and other delicious Filipino foods. The house buzzed with the chatter and laughter of aunts, uncles, and US-based cousins.

Despite the festive atmosphere, tension hung in the air as family members bickered over the quality of gifts and bustled around in a frenzy. As usual, I was a quiet spectator, absorbing the lively scene with detached amusement. However, my attention was drawn to one family member who seemed out of sorts that day. It was Lola Monica, the family matriarch, a figure I knew only through brief greetings and the various stories I had heard.

Lola, a strong Filipino grandmother who had raised 12 children through the trials of World War II and the subsequent loss of her husband in his fifties, seemed unusually disturbed. I watch her, her small, wrinkled hands moving feverishly as she writes something, a scowl of unease on her face. Suddenly, she called for silence, using Mamamon as her amplifier to quiet the noisy room. The family fell silent, turning their attention to Lola, who had something important to say.

At that moment, before she even spoke, I sensed that her words would be impactful.

When Lola began to talk, her presence filled the room. She spoke with Eva Peron's charisma and Martin Luther King's articulation, delivering a poignant and powerful message. Her speech, lasting seven minutes, was a raw and honest expression of her disappointment. She spoke of her disgust with the materialism overshadowing the true meaning of Christmas, urging the family to

318

focus on love and togetherness rather than gifts and petty arguments. Her words will forever haunt me, "It is all about love."

Through her words, I learned of her past-the struggles, the pain, the profound love, and her deep-seated desire for family unity. Her story was a tapestry of resilience, woven through years of hardship and loss, yet underscored by an unwavering commitment to her family. She spoke of raising her children alone, her challenges, and the strength she drew from her faith. Her speech made me rethink my priorities, questioning the importance I had placed on trivial matters.

Who would have thought this tiny, four-foot-nine -woman Filipina could make a six-foot black man feel so small and petty? Her strength was not just endearing; it was awe-inspiring. Her love was not just true; it was a force, a passionate, mighty heart beating within a small frame. That Christmas Eve, Lola Monica changed my perspective forever with her powerful words and indomitable spirit. In her, I saw the embodiment of true strength and unconditional love, a lesson in what truly matters in life."

-Joseph Baker (son-in-law)

Special Tribute for Mama

"It's hard to think of Lola. sitting here in a cold house, bundled up in a sweater. When I think of Lola, I think of humid air, and fresh fish, the sound of chicken and the whir of a fan. When I first met Lola, she was already in her 80's. stooped low, thinning gray hair, walking slowly. But when you looked into her eyes, you could see it all...harvesting coconuts, playing the piano, falling in love, being a mother. I remember sitting in her room, listening to her recount her memories of being a little girl and as a young mother during the war.

I loved hearing her stories-she was a walking museum carrying with her a rich history and the keen intellect to describe it in a meaningful way. She told stories of falling in love with a man she would stay true to until the very end. But mostly she told stories about her children. I can't imagine that raising twelve children afforded her much time to give each one individual love and encouragement; or that being a single mother after her husband passed away allowed her to think of much more than ensuring their survival. But the fierceness and pride that shone through her eyes when speaking of her children was never dulled by time or age.

When Lola spoke of the war, she described in vital detail hiding in the mountains with her babies-her need to protect her children overriding all else.

When she described what it was like after Lolo passed, she weaved a complicated tale of ensuring that each child was afforded an opportunity to not only survive but succeed-in older children caring for younger children, each child contributing in a meaningful way. But while she spoke with determination about her children, she spoke with not only pride, but a sense of joy for her grandchildren and great-grandchildren. In those children, she was able to step back (even if only slightly), to revel in their childhood.

And despite having a family large enough to constitute a small village in themselves, she knew all of her grandchildren. And when I say she knew them, she knew them. Not just their names and their parents and their siblings. She could pinpoint things about them that perhaps they didn't even know-their motivations and biggest dreams.

In short, when I think of Lola, I think of a force of nature. A woman who defied convention, who succeeded despite a million odds against her. A woman who not only listened, but heard. And while she is no longer with us, each one of her children, grandchildren, and great-grandchildren carry with them a piece of her- her ability to charm, her ability to hear, her ability to survive, and her ability to thrive."

By Elizabeth Young, JD (daughter in law)

My Personal Memories of Mama:
Simple Pleasures

Mama had a unique way of enjoying life's simple pleasures, and one of her favorite indulgences was checking into hotels during our vacations and reunions. It was a tradition she cherished, a time when she could relax, unwind, and savor the warmth of a cozy hotel room. But it wasn't just about the accommodations; it was the entire experience that brought her joy.

Her eyes would light up with anticipation as we approached the hotel, and she'd always have a twinkle in her eyes when we entered the lobby. Mama loved to be pampered, and she made sure to savor every moment of it. The hotel staff must have adored her because she had an uncanny ability to strike up genuine conversations with them. She'd engage in heartfelt exchanges, sharing stories and laughter with the people she encountered.

One of Mama's favorite moments during our hotel-hopping adventures was when we found ourselves by the beach. She had an undeniable affinity for beachfront hotels, and once we checked in, her face would light up with pure joy. She had a way of finding her own spot by the shoreline, where the gentle lapping of waves and the soothing sounds of nature provided her with a sense of tranquility like no other. As she sat there, gazing out at the endless expanse of sea and sky, her worries and cares simply melted away. The beach was her sanctuary, a place where she could find peace, recharge her spirit, and immerse herself in the beauty of the natural world.

One thing Mama never missed was the hotel's feedback form. She took those surveys seriously, offering her insights on the service, the food, and every aspect of her stay. It wasn't just a formality for her; it was an opportunity to ensure that others experienced the same comfort and hospitality she cherished.

Those hotel stays became more than just nights away from home; they were moments of pure delight, a chance for Mama to savor life's pleasures to the fullest.

Her love for these simple luxuries is a reminder that happiness can be found in the most unexpected places and that every experience, no matter how small, can be a source of joy.

Love for flowers and plants.

My mother had an extraordinary love for flowers and plants. Her garden was a testament to her green thumb and nurturing spirit. She took immense pleasure in tending to her garden, watching it bloom with vibrant colors and fragrant blooms.

She used to love it when my sister-in-law, Amai, created some beautiful flower arrangements from her garden every time she visited her in Moalboal. I remember how she would often explain to her helpers how to water the plants and the specific care each plant needed. Her garden was not just a collection of plants but a living testament to her boundless love for the beauty of nature."

CONCLUSION:

In the warm embrace of these heartfelt tributes, we see a tapestry woven with the threads of love, respect, and cherished memories. As we bid farewell to this chapter, it becomes abundantly clear that my mother, Moning, has left an indelible mark on each of us. Her legacy of love, resilience, and unwavering faith is a beacon that will continue to guide our lives.

As we close this book, let us not say goodbye to her memory, but rather, let us carry her spirit with us as we navigate the journey of life. Let us draw strength from her example and continue to honor her legacy by embracing the values she held dear; in our hearts, she lives on, and in our actions, her love endures. This memoir is not just a story of her life but a testament to the enduring impact of a mother's love. We are eternally grateful for the love, wisdom, and memories she shared with us, and we will carry them forward as we continue our own journeys. Let us pass down her legacy to the younger generations so they, too can be inspired by her example. May this memoir serve as a beacon of hope, a source of strength, and a reminder that love, faith, and family are the greatest treasures of life.

In honor of our beloved Mama and to carry forward her enduring legacy of love, strength, and resilience, our family is coming together for the "EMMO Sandalo Reunion", which will commence in just one month from now. As we gather for our upcoming reunion, a three-day celebration with love, laughter, and shared memories, we can't help but feel the absence of our beloved Mama. This will be the first reunion without her physical presence, but her spirits lives on in each of us, and her legacy is etched in our hearts. Mama may have left this world, but her spirit continues to guide us, and her love will forever be the foundation of our family.

May her memory be a blessing, and may her love continue to inspire us all.

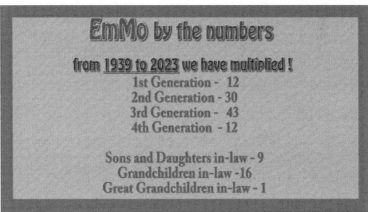

"From our parents' lineage, our family has flourished, embodying the enduring legacy of love and resilience passed down through generations."

Remembering the years....

Presented here are additional images capturing precious moments, including a particularly significant one featuring my father. Let's take a moment to appreciate and reflect on these treasured memories with our loved ones.

Our handsome father.

Moalboal

Life is not measured by the number of breaths we take but by the number of moments that take our breath away.
Mama at 95

The glue that holds us together, MAMA MONING at 95 yrs old.

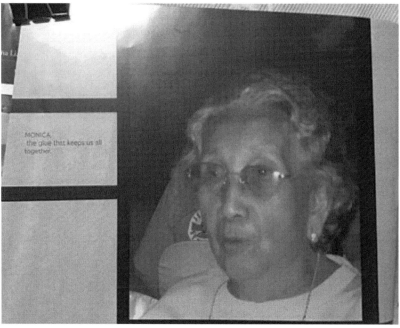

329

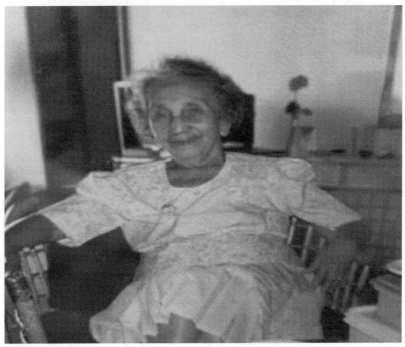

STRONGLY UNITED
25
2007
SANDALO FAMILY REUNION

ADDITIONAL DETAILS THAT I WOULD LIKE TO SHARE

MAMA'S CONCERNS:

I remember receiving a heartfelt letter from Mama, written in her elegant handwriting, that always made her words feel even more special. She was back home in the Philippines, and I was here in the US, thousands of miles apart, but always connected by the love she poured into every word.

In her letter, she asked about my children, reminiscing about how she cared for them during her visits when they were younger. But amidst the stories and updates, Mama's love and concern for her children, even in their adulthood, shone brightly.

She expressed her worries about her sons and their habit of consuming hard liquor, especially her oldest son, Leo who had some health challenges. Mama's maternal instincts were as strong as ever, and she couldn't help but fret over their health.

She confided in me, requesting that I, as a nurse, offer some advice to her boys. She hoped that maybe my words would carry a different weight, but she asked me not to reveal that it was her who had shared her concerns. It was a testament to Mama's enduring love and her unwavering commitment to the well-being of her family. Her love was a thread that bound us all, transcending time and distance."

-Rebecca Lopez-Golden (Author)

PRAYER FOR ALL MOTHERS

"Good and Gentle God, we pray in gratitude for our mothers and for all the women who have joined with you in the wonder of bringing forth new life. You who became human through a woman, grant to all mothers the courage they need to face the uncertain future that life with children always brings. Give them the strength to live and to be loved in return, not perfectly, but humanly. Give them the faithful support of husband, family and friends as they care for the physical and spiritual growth of their children. Give them joy and delight in their children to sustain them through the trials of motherhood. Most of all, give them the wisdom to turn to you for help when they need it most. Amen

MEMORIES

338

SYNOPSIS

*"In **Faith, Love and Family: Indomitable Spirit of a Mother and her Extraordinary Tale,** we delve into the extraordinary life of Monica Babiera Sandalo, a woman of indomitable spirit who navigated the tumultuous waters of war, widowhood, and motherhood with unwavering love and resilience. Set against the backdrop of World War II, Monica's story unfolds as she courageously raises 12 children single-handedly after the untimely death of her husband. Through heartaches and triumphs, Monica's unconditional love shines as a beacon of hope, guiding her family through adversity with strength and grace. **'Faith, Love and Family',** is a testament to the power of faith, maternal love, the enduring bonds of family, and the resilience of the human spirit."*

About The Author

Rebecca S. Lopez-Golden

As the sixth child in a family of twelve siblings, I've always felt like I held a unique position in the bustling Sandalo household. Growing up as a middle child, I discovered a sense of balance between the wisdom of my older siblings and the enthusiasm of my younger ones.

My journey led me to a fulfilling career in nursing, where I dedicated 55 years of my life to the noble profession of surgical nursing. Throughout my career, I've had the privilege of caring for countless patients and witnessing the miracles of healing firsthand.

Outside of my professional life, I am blessed with a loving family of my own. I am supported by my loving husband and our blended family, which includes my three wonderful children from my previous marriage and two grandchildren. My family has been my rock and my greatest source of joy.

A pivotal moment in my life occurred when I discovered my mother's diary after her passing. This treasure trove of memories and reflections sparked a newfound passion within me—a desire to honor my mother's legacy by sharing her remarkable story with the world. It was then that I knew I had found my calling as an author.

Now, as I embark on this new chapter of my life, I am excited to weave together the threads of my own experiences and those of my beloved mother into a tapestry of inspiration and resilience. Join me on this journey as we celebrate the power of faith, love, and family.

A LITTLE INFO ABOUT MOALBOAL, THE SANDALO'S HOMETOWN